Chantell Leonie Hayles

BEAUTY FOR ASH
© Copyright 2018 Cha[

ISBN: 978-0-244-96722-2

Chantell Leonie Hayles asserts the moral right to be identified as the author of this work. Unless otherwise indicated, all the Holy Scripture quotations are taken from the HOLY BIBLE.

New Living Translation (NLT)

Holy Bible, New Living Translation, copyright © 1996, 2004, 2007, 2013, 2015 by Tyndale House Foundation. Used by permission of Tyndale House Publishers Inc., Carol Stream, Illinois 60188. All rights reserved.

[First Edition]
Printed in the United States of America

Email: purposeinthepain.ministries@outlook.com

Front Cover Design by Chantell and Errol Hayles
Interior Layout Design by Daniele Luciano Moskal
Wedding Photograph by Simeon Thaw

© 2018 Chantell Leonie Hayles

ACKNOWLEDGEMENTS

$\mathbb{F}$irst and foremost, I would like to thank GOD. He is the true Author of my story. He writes every chapter of my life. I thank Him for His unconditional 'agape' love, His tender mercy, His patience, His caring compassion & great grace towards me. Without Him, none of this would be possible. I am in awe of Him daily, and will be eternally grateful for what He has done in my life, and other people's lives.

To my husband Errol, thank you for bearing and being patient with me as I took the time to focus on my book. Thank you for showing me what true love is. For your commitment to me. For never leaving me. For staying at the point where others left. For loving me unconditionally. You are truly special and I am so grateful to God for showing His love toward me by bringing you into my life. Thank you for sharing this life with me. **"I LOVE YOU ERROL!"**

Thank you to my beautiful daughter Siantae for giving me a reason to never give up. GOD'S timing is perfect, and HE brought you into my life at the perfect time. You are such a beautiful blessing, and I am thankful to the LORD that He allowed me to be your mummy.

To my mother who has always been there for me, supporting me when I had nothing, encouraging me through my pain and struggles and giving your best so that I would be okay. Thank you for all that you have done for me throughout my life. Thank you for your support with this book. I am grateful for you.

I am thankful to Abayomi "Saint" Bogle who initially first proof-read my manuscript, and helped me to get it into some kind of order. Without your help I would never have been able to make the improvements that you supported me with. Thank you for reading it without judgement. "God bless you!"

Thank you to my publisher and brother and friend in Christ, Daniele Luciano Moskal, who's valuable knowledge and expertise in the ministerial field of writing

& publishing brought everything to completion; who prayerfully supported me in achieving my dream to get this my baby: "BEAUTY for ASHES" book birthed, and in print world-wide. Thank you for your dedication to my book as if it were your own. "God bless you!"

Lastly, I sincerely thank you the reader for purchasing this book; for my prayer is the words found in this book will resonate with you that whatever you have faced or are facing right now in everyday life, there is One Very Important Special Person who loves everything about you, and specifically knows every single detail about your life - from the very moment you were born - Who is a very present help in any time of trouble - Who gave me a second chance, and a **'Purpose in the Pain'** ministry , for carrying on living in life today.........that person is the LORD Jesus Christ!!!

Chantell Leonie Hayles

CONTENTS

Pages 7-9...Introduction

Pages 10-25... In The Beginning

Pages 26-41...Innocence Lost

Pages 42-50...Dark Times

Pages 51-63...Suffering In Silence

Pages 64-75... When Anything Goes

Pages 76-85...Cursed In New York

Pages 86-101.............................Needle in a Haystack, the Lost Sheep

Pages 102-119...Season Of Rebellion

Pages 120-128..............................When The Past Comes to Haunt

Pages 129-138.............The End Is Only The Beginning In Disguise

Pages 139-152..Love Never Fails

Pages 153-179.....................When My Mess Became A Message

Pages 180-182.................................... Prayers Of Deliverance

Pages 183...............................Purpose in the Pain Ministries

INTRODUCTION

Dear Reader and beloved friend, I thank you for

allowing me to share my life, my testimonies; within this my very first book **"Beauty for Ashes"** with you. My prayer is that it will be a blessing to you, and hopefully it will encourage you to know there is a God who saw you – yes you! When you where housed in your mother's womb. **(Psalm 139: 13-16).** He knew WHO your father and mother would be, and what nations they would be born from. He knew you and the circumstances of your home, and where you would grow up. He knew all the schools you would attend and the neighbourhood, the country, the city, the town in which you would live. For God has given everyone here on planet earth the ability to survive and walk with you through all the good times and the bad ones. He has given you survival techniques and guardian angels to keep you and protect you in times of trouble **(Psalm 91:11).** He chose you – yes you! Before the foundation of the world He chose you to be holy and without any blame before Him in love **(Ephesians 1:4).** He cries with you when you cry, and He laughs with you when you laugh! He grieves for you when you are misunderstood and treated unfairly! He is watching and waiting, and so looking forward to the day when you – yes you would receive Jesus as your LORD and Saviour, for He longs for your sweet fellowship, desiring you – yes you to know Him more and more intimately! Yes, my survival techniques are probably different than yours. Whatever they are, and whatever your life may be up to this point of purchasing and reading this book, the peace of God can change all the deep painful regrets, and all the damaging, hurtful emotional wounds of your past experiences into a heart of thanksgiving and praise, I am a living testimony to God's unconditional love, and amazing great grace in changing a person like me from the inside to the outside, and give them a much needed second chance; for there is **'BEAUTY for ASHES!'** There is **'PURPOSE IN THE PAIN!'**

You can experience victory and freedom – you no longer need to fear or be a victim of the past- today is a brand new day, and whether your "trouble or struggle" is rejection, fear of death or loss of a loved one, abandonment, pornography, masturbation, depression, a business failure, unemployment, low-self-esteem, a mental disorder, lust, a chemical imbalance, a marriage problem, a child who maybe is in a strange land of drugs and alcohol and sex, financial disaster or anything else, I want to encourage you God loves you and can perform miracles, signs and wonders. For nothing is impossible for God to do; if God can turn around my promiscuous wayward life-style, and emotional pain and damage of rejection, hurt and anger, to give me freedom and victory - He most certainly can do it for you, in Jesus Christ's loving and faithful name, **AMEN & AMEN & AMEN!!!**

Chantell Leonie Hayles

DISCLAIMER:

Some names and identifying details in this book have been changed to protect the privacy of individuals.

Chapter 1
IN THE BEGINNING

My name is Chantell Leonie Hayles, and I was born

near the second biggest city named Birmingham on the 8th of September, 1984, at West Bromwich in a district town named Sandwell in the West Midlands, an area known as the 'Black Country'. My family surname was Douglas; as my earthly parents whom the good LORD used to birth me into this world were of Jamaican/British heritage. Although, the majority of my personal life has not been plain sailing, nor has it been nice, or easy – it has first and foremost in all truthfulness been a very bumpy 'rollercoaster ride'. A rocky ride, that has seen me derail off the main tracks of life many times; an emotional up and down ride that witnessed me drag, weigh, and pull me down with many overloaded emotional, mental, physical, spiritual, and financial burdens – burdens that were full of troubles, traumatic pain, cataract tears, fearful anguish, tragic loss and shattering brokenness, that gave me by God's grace new understanding, as to why I am here on planet earth, and to praise the LORD, for keeping me safe under His protective care and security through the times were I would not have made it otherwise. Unfortunately, I don't remember too much about growing up as a young child; all I can recollect is I somehow knew I had been born into a big family, in which my mother was one of ten children. My mother and father had sadly separated just after I was born. She had met my sister's dad when I was still a baby. My sister Cyan was born when I was almost 4 years of age. As I grew up, I would spend a lot of time playing out on the street with my friends in all kinds of weather. This was the era where young children used to be out in the parks, or playing **'knock-down-ginger'**; this was a cheeky game that involved knocking on the front door (or ringing the doorbell) of a victim, then **running** away before the door could be answered. The name knock-down-ginger or **knocky** door ginger, used in Britain, comes from a British poem: *'Ginger, Ginger broke a winder. Hit the winda – crack!'* Bike riding, climbing trees and just generally being children was the norm back then. It was also the era where mobile phones didn't confine us to our rooms, or computer consoles didn't confine us to the Television sets. This was an era where we could simply and playfully enjoy being children. During and living out my childhood years, one thing I probably and desperately sought after passionately was a loving affirmation of any kind or description; I always craved attention. And, you as the reader of this book will graciously confirm it too, that in all honesty you, and I, and every living person that has breath on planet earth is wanting some kind of attention or affirmation. I'm not sure why I felt this way; maybe it was to do with the fact that I didn't have my earthly father around long enough (even though my sister's father was around). I just always longed for the love and attention of my own earthly father, but hardly ever got it because by this time my father had left, and was now subsequently living in London, while I lived with my mother in Birmingham; so he didn't visit me too often.

All that I ever wanted at that age was to be loved and accepted, yet I felt so alone, I felt unwanted; I pondered over-and-over again in my mind, and kept asking myself the same question many a time: *"Why I wasn't good enough for my father?"*. I knew that my mother loved me but it wasn't enough for me. I deeply wanted so much to be hugged by my earthly biological father, and to be told that I was everything to him. I felt insecure. My esteem as a young child was very low at this point, and the only way I could deal with it personally was to somehow, some way, begin to tackle this issue head on by seeking attention at home, or at school. Sadly and woefully, I got into trouble a lot in my primary school years by causing a lot of problems for the teachers; my mother sadly had to go to the school on numerous occasions because I had gotten into trouble yet again! I even got suspended from school one day for physically attacking one of my classmates because some boys fancied her, yet nobody fancied me. Even at such a young tender age, I was battling the grips of jealousy of other girls. The teachers gave me the label of a school bully, and I wore that derogative label like a gold chain around my neck. I accepted the label because just like everyone else, I didn't think highly of myself. When I moved into year 4, I had Mr. Turner who I named 'the teacher from hell!' I remember this particular teacher didn't like me one bit. He always used to single me out for no apparent reason at all. One particular day, after having a day off, I brought a note into him from my mother, explaining why I wasn't present the day before. This note had been written on a small piece of lined paper which she had torn out of a notebook. When I handed it to Mr. Turner; right in front of the whole class he screwed it up, threw it on the floor and demanded I explain what was written in the note. He said that his reason for this was because it wasn't written on an inappropriate piece of paper. The following day, my mother visited the school to complain to the head teacher on how Mr. Turner was treating me. Not much was done though! This teacher continued to make my life a misery, and it started to take its toll on me. At the age of approximately 9 years, I started to wet my bed and started to suffer the symptoms of OCD. [**Obsessive-compulsive disorder** (OCD) is a mental disorder in which people have unwanted and repeated thoughts, feelings, ideas, sensations (obsessions), and behaviors that drive them to do something over and over (compulsions). Often the person carries out the behaviors to get rid of the obsessive thoughts.]

I began touching things more than once to make four. If

I was out with friends – I would suddenly realise that I had left the bike cupboard open; I would feel or sense a strange horrible feeling inside until I would have to go all the way back home just to shut it. I didn't realise at that time that it was obsessive compulsive disorder (OCD) until many years later in my teenage years. I remember every time that my hand would touch something by accident; I would have to touch it another 3 times to make 4. And, then when it got really bad, I would do 4 sets of 4. It quickly started to take over my life and I unfortunately had no control over it. I felt like a slave to this act, and I didn't have any strength to stop what I was doing. I was just a little girl. In between playing with my Barbie dolls and playing out with my friends, I was touching things over and over again, up to 100 times a day! I was ashamed about what I was doing. That's something that the devil likes to do, make us do something bad - then he'll make us feel ashamed whilst were doing it - but God is much bigger than our shameful secrets, and if we share our burdens we are able then to disarm the enemy. I don't know what finally made me pluck up the courage to tell someone but I remember the day that I told my step-father, Joe. I always saw my sister's dad Joe as my hero, and felt that if anyone would be able to help me stop what I was doing, it was him. My words to him were: ***"Joe, I keep touching things over and over again and I don't know why, but I can't stop?"***. He said to me that I just had to get over what I was doing. I didn't have the strength to just "get over what I was doing"; so as you may have guessed, Joe's words didn't help me much. I just continued to do this daily and allow it to control my life. As a young child under the age of 10, OCD wasn't the only thing that I struggled with. Unknown to anybody, I was also struggling with the desires of lust and masturbation, maybe it grew from a desperation of wanting to be loved as I felt unloved. They do say that it is a form of 'self love'. I really don't remember the age that it started but I do know it started, and it was something that I struggled with for many years later, even into my adult Christian life, and it was one of the hardest things that I have had to overcome. Even through all of these problems, I would always pray. I don't know what made me start praying as I hadn't been brought up or around religion, and I'd only attended church a few times for Sunday school. For some reason in my mindset, I always knew that there was a God, and I used to speak to Him throughout my childhood. Somehow, He seemed like the closest person to me, the only person that I felt really understood me. I often get asked the question, why at that point did I assume God was a He (masculine), and not feminine? In my heart I just felt that God was the Father that I longed for. The one I could be myself with, and tell all my fears and problems and anxieties too like a real human father. Whenever I spoke to God, I always felt comforted. I remember my sister laughing when I told her this, but my prayers always ended like this: *"I love you, me, Your Family, my family, Your people in your world and my people in my world!"*. My prayers felt very personal and intimate; I always knew that I was praying to someone that heard me and understood me.

When I was 11, my beloved mother decided that we were going to live in Bolton, a town in Greater Manchester, in the North West of England, with my step-dad which I was quite excited about. A few months before we were meant to move out, my sister was hit by a car and injured very badly. She had bleeding on her brain, and the doctors didn't think that she would make it overnight, but when Gods hand is on someone's life, nothing can stop what He has planned and predestined! She was unconscious and on a life support machine for many months. During this time, I'm not sure what I honestly thought but one thing I know for sure, that I wanted my sister to get better and recover fully from her ordeal. My mother practically lived in the hospital, and I saw from a close viewpoint the devastating, emotional, mental, spiritual and physical effects of having a very ill child was having on her health and whole wellbeing. I had to stay with my family and continue to live as normal whilst my sister was fighting for her life from a hospital bed. My beloved sister was in hospital for 2 months, 2 weeks and 2 days and came out on my mother's birthday. When she came out of the hospital, we all moved to Bolton to live with Joe. I thought that I would love it but I hated it! To move from a big city to what feels like a small village, was definitely not what I was hoping for. I was made to feel like an alien in a foreign place that had hardly any other black people. And, it was during this time, when I was in my final year of primary school that I also got targeted and racially bullied and picked upon for my thick lips, of my skin colour and because I had a Birmingham accent! I was simply targeted because I was different. I already felt like an outsider in my childhood years because my sister's father wasn't my real dad (even though he always treated me like I was his), and I felt even more of an outsider when I was living in Bolton. Too many times whilst living in Bolton, I wished that I was someone else*.........."Maybe if my hair was blonde, maybe if I was white, maybe if I had smaller lips and spoke with a Northern accent, maybe then I would feel accepted?'* I remember trying to force myself to speak with a Bolton accent, I wish I never tried too because I actually sounded Irish, (anything just too simply fit in with the status-quo!). I used to try and make my lips look smaller by pulling them into my mouth, just so others could accept me.

I hated everything about myself by this time, I felt like I wanted to be a different person and started feeling more and more jealous of other girls that I felt looked a lot better than me. I remember the day my mother told us all, that she was splitting up with my step-dad and that we were returning back to Birmingham. This was only a year after us moving to Bolton. It was bittersweet moment for me. I was so happy that we were moving back to Birmingham that I didn't even imagine how leaving my step dad would affect me. He was the only man in my life at this time as my father, had moved from London to New York permanently. At first, moving away didn't affect me much because I was busying myself with starting my new Secondary school which was a mixed comprehensive school called Queensbridge, in Moseley, Birmingham. After a few months I started to really miss Joe because even though he wasn't my real dad, Joe was the closest thing I had to having a real dad, and too me Joe was my Champion, my Hero. He always introduced me to people as his daughter, and he never made me feel unwelcome in any way, shape or form. Joe was perfect in my eyes. Being in my school in

Birmingham was the first time that I ever remember getting attention off any guys. It felt nice to feel wanted by someone of the opposite sex, and even though no one tried to pursue anything with me, it was just nice to see people showing me interest. Guys would often talk to me, and I had friends coming up to me telling me privately that certain guys at school fancied me. For someone that was continuously and repeatedly bullied for being different, it was a breath of fresh air to finally feel acknowledged and wanted. Two months after starting my new school, my mother announced that we were moving back to Bolton. 'Why?' you may ask (hmm yes that's what I thought too). She said that she felt more comfortable in Bolton and that we were moving into our own 2 bedroom house. *"Maybe this is a way that I can see more of Joe again?"* I thought. So I reluctantly packed my personal belongings and said good-bye to all my new friends that I had made. Moving back to Bolton was exactly how I had remembered it. BORING! That along with having to deal with the mundane boredom, I would undoubtedly have to put up with getting teased for my big lips again! When we moved back to Bolton I was still in my first year at Secondary school. At this point, as

I mentioned in the previous page, I started to take a shining to the opposite sex, even though they never took a shining to me. Whilst my friends were having boyfriends, I was just happy to finally have friends. I had a couple of friends that in between teasing me, they were actually very nice to me. So I just accepted the life that I had, and tried to simply get on with it.

During this period of time, I was still suffering from the desires of lust which I struggled daily with to stop. Female masturbation is a taboo subject, something that people don't talk about. Over the years I've come to realise that when it comes to men these things are expected and there's valuable support out there, if Christian men want to stop this whilst waiting until marriage. There doesn't seem or there isn't much help out there for Christian women that do struggle with this, and because of this we hold it in our secret caves (mindsets), and struggle with the shame alone. As it started as a young child, its hold on me got stronger as I got older, so when I became a Christian I accepted that it was a part of me that I shouldn't talk about, and instead become a slave to it. I now know that it's not something to be ashamed of, and that it's important to share this because a friend once told me that the detail that I don't share could be the element that changes one person's life – and just to know that someone else has struggled with the same thing. As well as this, I was also still struggling with obsessive compulsive disorder (OCD) and I remember the day I found out my problem and its name. I was at home. I was about 13 years old and lying in bed and a programme came on TV. All I remember was the lady saying something about OCD, and that she had to touch things more than once to make 3. That was all that I needed to hear, I ran into my mum's bedroom crying, screaming, that I finally knew what it was that I had. It was a huge relief to know the name of the condition that I was suffering from. In fact it was a huge relief to know that what I was doing was an actual condition and that I wasn't alone. I can't remember what my mum said to me that day but all I know is that even after finding out what it was that I had, because I didn't seek any help for this, I still continued to do this until later on in my life. Every weekend we used to travel to Birmingham from Bolton, and I remember I met a boy that I really liked. He quickly became my boyfriend, and I recall having my first kiss with him under a canal bridge at the age of 13. I thought I was in love, but then he dumped me for another friend of mine in Birmingham! I was heartbroken and I feel this contributed to my growing lack of trust in men, which, sadly for me, unfortunately followed me until very later on in life. After 2 years of living in Bolton, my mother dropped another bombshell. She told my sister and me, that we were moving back to Birmingham because she missed her own mother and father. I can't say that I wasn't happy because I was, and I kind of knew it was going to happen as we had a family rail ticket and were using it to travel to Birmingham EVERY weekend without fail. The only problem to me was that I didn't think I was ready for Birmingham, after all, because all my friends had lost their virginity and I felt that I needed to lose mine so that I would be ready for when I got a boyfriend in Birmingham even though I was still only 14 years of age. It sounds silly now but at that time, I felt that I didn't want the Birmingham boys to think that I was frigid. So subsequently, I remember the very day that I had planned to lose my virginity - I found a boy that I wanted to lose it to, and he made no complaints. I remember that night like it was yesterday, I had it all planned. I stayed at my friend Carmen's that particular day, and she sorted everything out for me, even where me and this guy were going to do the act (even though I don't call a park climbing frame the ideal place for your first time). She told this guy that he needed protection; then everything was sorted until it finally came to the time to do it, and I completely bailed out. I just couldn't go through with it. So we finally moved to Birmingham with my virginity still intact, but not for long.

Chapter 2
INNOCENCE LOST

Shortly after moving to Birmingham, I soon made some

friends and I was really enjoying my new life. I started going to a school not far from my house and I quickly became good friends with a girl called Sara. I was so desperate to fit in that I would lie to my friends by saying that I was sexually active. However, my plan backfired. Instead of making them like me, it made them dislike me. In the end I had to own up that I had lied, and that I had done it just to fit in with everyone. After this blatant lie, everyone seemed to accept me, or so it appeared. Sara and I were close friends, and every morning we would meet and walk to school together. There was one particular day that we were en route to school and we passed the most gorgeous boy. He was tall, dark and handsome and he had a captivating smile that drew me in. I couldn't get him out of my mind after that, and I was adamant that when we saw him next that Sara *had* to get his number for me. A few days later we passed this gorgeous stranger once again, so I asked Sara to get his number for me whilst I nervously stood about 2 metres away. I remember he wrote his number onto the palm of Sara's hand, she came over to me and I typed it in my mobile phone and then I nervously wrote my number on her other palm which she presented to him. It was all a bit childish but I was only 14 - and had never properly been involved with a guy before. Once this was all over and we had gotten over the embarrassment of our exchanging numbers, Leroy, (the gorgeous stranger), and I went our separate ways. I remember he called me the same night (I had to go out the room because I didn't want my mum to hear the conversation that I was having with him because as far as she was concerned, I wasn't allowed to have a boyfriend). He told me that he thought that I was a nice girl, and he asked me out right there and then on the phone. I enthusiastically said yes, and the month of April, 1999, was the first time I had a boyfriend. Our first kiss followed shortly after and I was totally smitten with him. Two months after meeting him, I decided that he was the one I was going to lose my virginity too; and after my painful first experience, we didn't do it again until 2 months after that. Losing my virginity at that time was wrong, I was only 14 years of age but it made me feel accepted and wanted. Even though I didn't realise it at the time, I now know that I subconsciously came to the dangerous conclusion in my head – that this was the way to be accepted by men, and that using my body would give me the attention that I so strongly felt that I lacked and needed.

I can recall the way my mum found out that I had a boyfriend; it was shortly after my 15th birthday in September, 1999 and Leroy had bought me a golden chain. We had an argument on this particular day, and I told him to "get lost". After I reached home, there was knock at the front door my mum went to answer it. When I heard Leroy's voice in the background I shook with fear, wondering what it was that he was saying to my mother, and for the fact that my mum would now know the truth - that I had a boyfriend. I wanted the ground to open up and swallow me whole, there and then. She stormed up the stairs, shouted at me and then told me that Leroy wanted his chain back. I reluctantly handed her the chain, and then quickly went to bed whilst she went to give it back to Leroy. No further discussion was had. However, the next day she came to me and asked if he was my boyfriend, which I confirmed he was. She then said something along the lines of him being "sweet" and that she "liked him", and that now I was "allowed to have a boyfriend". From then on Leroy and I were inseparable, seeing each other every day and spending all of our time together. I feel bad now, but I remember lying to my mum and saying that I was going ice skating with my friends, when really I was with Leroy, either at his house drinking cans of cider or getting up to some sexual activity in a park somewhere, or in his mums car. It was about a year later, and after exploring my new found sexual side with Leroy, that I decided that I wanted to 'see what other guys were like' (as I called it), as I didn't feel total satisfaction having attention from just one guy. I decided there and then, that Leroy and I no longer had a future and that I wanted to get out there in the big wide world, and enjoy other guys. We soon broke up and I felt free to give my body away to whoever wanted it. This soon started to become painful for me because even though it was my decision to start *linking* other boys (as we called it then), my heart longed for more than sex, and the more my heart longed for that something extra, that something special, the more men I would give my body to in the hope that I would get more from them. This spiraled out of control and I soon developed a bad name for myself locally. I concluded that Leroy was the only one that ever loved me, so I ended up getting back with him. Shortly after getting back with Leroy I remember Joe coming to Birmingham to see us. He had a brief discussion with my mother and I knew something was up. He didn't tell us there and then, all he said to my sister and I, was that he was taking us for a drive. Once in the car, Joe informed us that he will soon be moving to Canada for a year with work, and that he would be back the year later. I was really taken aback by it all, I didn't want Joe to go, and I knew that I would miss him too much!

"Who would be my hero now?!!!"

I remember being terrified when I was younger whilst watching the film 'Jurassic Park', a 1993 movie that was brilliantly directed by Steven Spielberg and starring the actors Sam Neill, Laura Dern, Jeff Goldblum, and Richard Attenborough. The Dinosaurs really scared me but I used to always think that if Dinosaurs ever came back into existence, that Joe would be the hero and save us all (yes, I know that it sounds ridiculous now but that's truly what I thought). So when Joe announced that he was going, I cried inconsolably. The only small comfort was that he said that he will contact us every day. That day Joe left, he didn't contact us again for 4 years! The grief was indescribable! Soon after, I experienced one of the biggest incidents which would govern my life up until this present day – Panic Attacks. I remember when the first one happened; I had lied to my mother and told her that I was staying with a friend when really I was going to stay with Leroy at his friend's house. The week before, I had done the same thing and gotten away with it, so I thought that I would do it again. Whilst at his friends house, Leroy and his friend were smoking skunk (Cannabis – skunk is a stronger type.)

As a curious teen, I decided that I wanted to take a drag to see what it was like. Shortly after taking my first drag I remember sitting there and feeling detached from my body, then everything went black. The next thing I remember is screaming that I'm dying! I can't remember much as I kept blacking out, but what I do remember is running outside the house as a car was pulling up. I recall opening the back door of the car, jumping in and saying that I was dying! I begged the driver to take me to a hospital. Leroy jumped in the car after me, and I wrote the number for my mother on his hand and said to him that if I die, to tell my mother that I'm sorry. I later found out that the car I jumped into was a taxi (which none of us called), and I truly believe to this very day that God by His precious timely Holy Spirit sent that taxi to the house for me. I really thought that I was dying; I had never experienced in my whole life the feeling that I was experiencing that particular cold winter's night in the car. My head was making a weird buzzing sound (or at least I thought it was). When we reached the hospital, Leroy paid the fare, and then we both got out of the car and ran into Dudley Road Accident & Emergency Ward. I remember saying to the lady on reception that I was dying, whilst she just sat there having a telephone conversation and completely ignoring me. When she eventually gave me her attention, she took a few details and then asked me to take a seat and wait for someone to call me. When we sat down I started to calm down a bit, but I was shaking uncontrollably. After what seemed like forever, a doctor eventually called me into a small room and immediately told me that I was having a panic attack, and that I wasn't actually dying - which was a huge relief to me (and Leroy for that matter). The doctor took some blood samples after I owned up to smoking cannabis, and he came back a short while later to say that there were no other drugs in my system except for the skunk which I had smoked. They also said that they would need to contact my mother. I begged them not to tell her what I had taken. Whilst the hospital contacted my mum, Leroy and I made up a lying story about how and while I was at my friend's house, I had suddenly, and without warning had a panic attack! I stated that Leroy played the caring boyfriend and came to get me and take me to hospital. My mum actually bought that story - which was a relief - as I wasn't up to explaining why I had decided to try smoking or why I had lied about staying with my friend for that matter. It wasn't until years later after becoming a born again Christian that I decided that it is important that I confess this to my mother, so I finally told her the truth. Thankfully she was okay about it. After going back home with my mum, I thought that would be the last time I would ever experience anything like that again. I could not have been anymore wrong.

Approximately only after a year-and-a-half after getting together; I and Leroy finally broke up for good. I don't even remember the reason why we decided to part ways but for me, it was a good thing because, once again, I wanted to experience other men and what they were like. So once again, I was giving myself to any man that would have me, in exchange for attention and affirmation. This wasn't getting me very far, as I realised every boy would pretend that they liked me just to get what they wanted from me. I decided that I really wanted to get back with Leroy, but by this time he had a new girlfriend but he still continued to sleep with me. Keeping this dirty secret I felt like I had power over him, and I had no problem with telling his new girlfriend what was going on as I wanted every girl to hurt like me. This was not a good idea on my part, as I didn't think of the nasty and evil consequences doing something like this could have in the long run. This girl soon found out my telephone number AND what school I attended - details which she could have only got from Leroy. Then one particular day, this girl and about 50 of her friends turned up outside my school to beat me up but thankfully, my teachers would not allow me to leave until they had gone.

What had I gotten myself into?

I soon realised that these girls were not remotely ever going to give up trying to get to me to give me a hard time. I was right because one day I had only walked to my friend Tanisha's house and I received a phone call off this girl to say that they had my little sister, and that they were not going to let her go until I had told them where I was. Reluctantly, I told them my whereabouts, and a whole tribe of women turned up outside Tanisha's house to beat me up. Tanisha's mum called my mother, and I remember nervously shaking with fear – patiently waiting inside the house until my mother turned up. When she arrived, she ordered me to come outside and said that there was no way that these girls were going to touch me whilst she was there so, feeling protected, I came outside to a flock of angry young women. As we started walking home I remember them behind us, breathing threats about next time they see me I won't be so lucky to have my mother with me, and how and what they were going to do to me next time they see me without my mother. About a month later I remember the day that these girls finally caught up with me. I was on the bus going to see my aunts, and a couple of these girls got on the bus. I was sat upstairs and I was by myself; so as far as they were concerned it was the perfect opportunity for them. They started to argue with me and then one of them tried to hit me from the side. The bus driver stopped the bus and escorted them all off the bus, leaving me shaken and quite embarrassed. It is with discomfort that I recall the second time these girls caught up with me; it is as clear today as it was the day it happened. I was in Birmingham City Centre, previously shopping and having lunch with one of my friends at the time; and standing at the bus stop I was suddenly surrounded by approximately 30 girls. Before I could properly assess the situation, one of them hit me with an umbrella, and then another girl trying to drag me to the floor. Suddenly, and without warning, one of the girls came toward me and bit a whole chunk out of my face; I remember screaming and then running across the road into a jewelry store where they called the police. The officers took a load of pictures and proceeded to find these girls. After this, my social life became none-existent as my mother was afraid to let me leave the house for fear of my safety. I was afraid of these girls and what they might do to me. It wasn't a way I wanted to live but it unfortunately became my life. Every time I left my house, for the fear of the unknown uncertainty of my daily life now, I would be constantly looking over my shoulders just waiting for these girls to pounce again. At one point, whilst away; they wrote on our white front door in black marker pen stating that they will soon get me. The embarrassment of having to scrub that door on a quiet cul-de-sac area in front of my neighbours certainly took its toll on me. I cried constantly and was on edge every time our front door bell rang. The panic attacks also got worse, and I started experiencing very vivid dreams about God and the devil. I also started to be afraid to sleep alone, so I slept with my mother every night as it was the only way that I felt safe. I began losing touch with reality. Everything that I was going through took its toll on my mental health. I refused to take any sort of painkillers or medication; for anything associated with them would bring about my panic attacks that I had previously encountered. It was a *drug* in the very first place that had simply caused me to have my first initial panic attack, so I started seeing all substances in the same light. I remember one day I had a terrible migraine headache, and my mother told me to take a paracetamol so, reluctantly, I did. About half an hour after taking it my mind started to play tricks on me, by telling me that I had just taken a drug and that it was going to have the same effect as the skunk. Because of these thoughts I caused myself to have a major panic attack. I started screaming at my mum to phone the ambulance, insisting I was dying, and that I needed immediate medical attention! This was a very scary experience for both my mother and me. I felt like I was completely losing my mind, and I can't imagine how my mother felt seeing her (then 15 year old daughter), act this way. My mother eventually called the ambulance when she realised that she wasn't going to get me to calm down. By the time the ambulance had arrived, I had calmed down however, they still decided to take me in as my blood pressure was high (hypertension). After a night in the hospital, I was allowed home. Weeks later, it happened a second time, and once again I was admitted into hospital for the night. During all these occurrences, I started seeing even more guys as I thought that maybe if I found someone to love me, maybe the pain of what was going on in my life would finally stop. I craved the attention of men like an addict craves drugs. I would be constantly jumping on the bus going to link different men and allow them to sleep with me. I was still yet to learn that giving me, myself to guys only added to the pain as none of them wanted a lasting relationship with me. Sleeping with men wasn't about me wanting to sleep around, I just longed for someone to accept me. Giving my body to a guy (just so that he could love and accept me for even one night), made me feel like I was worth something. I was so empty, anything to fill this void that I felt in my heart. I prayed to God, but at that time I knew nothing about Jesus Christ of Nazareth, and how He bore my sins that I could be free from this emptiness. All this, plus the stress of my forthcoming school exams just made the panic attacks escalate. I became paranoid that people were poisoning my food. These suspicions got so bad that I wouldn't allow my mum to cook for me or anyone to make me a drink as I started to believe that they would spike me. Thinking back now, I realise how irrational that sounds. I know my beloved mother; the mother who birthed me in her womb for nine months would never hurt me, but at that time my paranoia was real, and I didn't trust anybody. I have no doubt that I was actually losing my mind. My GP decided to refer me to a psychiatrist, but after attending one session I decided not to go back because I was convinced that only mad people spoke to psychiatrists, and I didn't want people to think that I was mad! Once again, after taking another paracetamol tablet for a headache, I ended up in hospital for a 3rd time with another bad panic attack. By this time my paranoia became hypochondria, and I was fully convinced that I had a brain tumor. Whilst in the hospital I shared my concerns with the hospital staff and demanded a brain scan, which of course they refused. I was convinced that this brain tumor must be the cause of everything that was happening to me! I didn't have a brain tumor; but this was my third panic attack in less than a year. This time was much different though. I remember a social worker came to speak to me one day whilst I was on the Children's Ward, and what she said to me stuck with me long after she said it. She told me that I really need to sort myself out, and warned me that if I was a couple of months older, they would have put me straight into a psychiatric hospital. That really scared me as I didn't feel that I was mad but I knew I had a lot of issues that needed dealing with. I made a promise to myself there and then that I would not end up in hospital with panic attacks again. Little did I realise was that the panic attacks and the physical attacks were only the beginning of my problems. My life was about to get much darker.

Chapter 3
DARK TIMES

I missed Joe terribly; I really don't know why he chose

not to contact my sister and me. She was his 'Princess', and was really close to her dad. He must not have appreciated how he almost lost her to the road accident many years ago. He failed to keep his promise to us. That being said, I still loved him very much. My sister didn't talk about him often but one thing she did say was that she wasn't' interested in him. I was the opposite, I couldn't get over the fact that he didn't call us… didn't he *love* us? I remember one day after school I was sat in my mother's room, and I just broke down in uncontrollable tears asking my mum why Joe didn't love me and my sister anymore. I was heartbroken and I felt rejected by someone that I loved dearly. All these thoughts made me come to unhealthy conclusions about men. I just wanted one man to love me. Why did my dad leave? Why did my step-dad leave? Was it my fault? I felt that no one would ever love me; I felt that I was destined to be by myself forever because as far as I was concerned, men didn't stay! During all of this, my dreams became even more vivid. I started to dream more again about the devil and God. I remember having a dream that I was sat on a floor and Satan was next to me, and he tried to cover me in his cloak. I also had many dreams about the world ending, and of Jesus Christ coming back. I started to wonder to myself what all this meant as I wasn't a religious person and didn't know much about Jesus Christ of Nazareth - except my belief that He existed. I told my dad's mother about all my dreams as she was a born again Christian, and she said that she believed that God was calling me into a relationship with Him. I decided to ignore the calling as I wasn't entirely sure about it all and what it meant. What I do know is that the dreams became more and more vivid as time went on. I remember having a dream that I was walking down a dark tunnel and I could see a light at the end, and as I started to walk toward this amazing bright light I heard a voice say to me: '*I'm not ready for you yet*' , and then I woke up out of my sleep feeling very strange. Apart from the dreams, I was having very weird and terrifying experiences in my sleep. There were many times that I would feel a sense of waking up or being awake but not being able to move my body - feeling paralysed. This happened many times.

W hen I turned 16, nothing changed. I was still living a

very promiscuous lifestyle; I was still suffering from panic attacks; I was still getting attacked by the girls whenever they saw me, and I still wasn't allowing anybody to cook or prepare food or drink for me as I thought that they would spike me! When it came to the time for us to do our GCSE school exams, I remember having to be taken out of the examination hall because I had a panic attack. After doing our exams I then met a boy that I really liked, I soon became smitten with him. I got on well with his family, and his mother even got me a job at the McDonalds where she worked. The thing is, I would get a phone call off his ex-girlfriend every now and then to say that he was cheating on me with her. This definitely put a strain on our relationship as I didn't trust him one bit, but I tried to force myself to believe him when he said that he wasn't cheating because I didn't want to lose him. I didn't want to be by myself, he was like a breath of fresh air in my life and I wasn't willing to give that up just because someone said that he was cheating. I was grateful just to have someone even if it did mean that he would cheat on me. In my eyes I wasn't worth much anyway so didn't expect much for myself. One day during the summer time of 2001, we had to go to school to do one final exam. After finishing the exam, I started to take the 20 minutes walk back home with my best friend Sara. Oddly, Sara said that she didn't like the coat that she was wearing. It was a nice denim jacket, and I had a little thin black jacket on, so I agreed to swap coats with her. As we neared my friend Tanisha's house, I saw her standing outside. Tanisha had stayed at my house a couple days before, and I truly believed she was my friend, but for some reason this day was different. I actually can't remember what she said; all I remember is her starting an argument with me. Then her younger sister came out and they both started shouting and arguing with me. All of a sudden without provocation, both began physically attacking me. I felt like I had to fight for my life against two girls, so I lashed out and I punched Tanisha in the face, which resulted in me breaking her nose.

Realising she was hurt, they both retreated into their house. I went into my friend Janet's house next door, and we where trying to make sense as to why Tanisha and Simone wanted to fight me when I actually thought that they were my friends. I later decided to go to the chip shop up the road with Sara so that she could get some food. As we left the chip shop and neared Tanisha's house again, Simone and another girl came outside. They jumped me, and with my back turned, I didn't see Tanisha come out of her house with a large bread knife. All I felt next was the weirdest sensation in my back, I quickly turned around to witness Tanisha stood there with a knife in her hand dripping with blood - *My blood.* I didn't know what to do so I just ran. I ran back to Janet's house and her mum called the ambulance, and my mother. By the time my mother had arrived, the paramedics were already with me so they took me to the hospital. After assessing me, the doctors informed me that I had quite a deep wound to my back about a centimeter from my spine. They also stated that the denim jacket that I was wearing saved my life because of how thick it was. I knew then that it wasn't the jacket that saved my life but that it was an intervention by God! It was Him that caused me to swap jackets with Sara just before getting stabbed. Even though I acknowledge God's goodness, I still refused to start living for Him at that time. After stitching up my wound, the hospital kept me in overnight for observation.

Less than a week after getting stabbed whilst still wrapped in hospital bandages, I decided to go to a christening with my friend Cheryl and a couple other friends, near where my boyfriend lived; but he couldn't attend as he had to go to work. I felt that I needed to cheer myself up after the events of the previous week. When I got there, I remember feeling a bit uncomfortable, as I saw one of the girls there that attacked me on the bus before, but because she wasn't with all her friends I felt a bit better. The only problem was she was with a completely new bunch of girls and she kept whispering to them. From their body language, she was obviously saying something about me. Despite this, I tried to enjoy myself at the christening with my friends and then when it finished we called a taxi to go home. When the taxi arrived we got into it, then suddenly, these girls surrounded the car. We quickly locked the doors and as the taxi driver started to pull off I remember them pulling at the door handles, 2 of them jumping onto the bonnet of the moving car, like they would do in an action movie. I remember feeling a sudden feeling of intense fear. I shouted to the taxi driver advising him to brake suddenly so that they could fall off but instead he slowed the car down. All of a sudden all the car doors swung open and I remember my friends and the taxi driver being pulled out of the car. Suddenly all these girls where coming in from different directions trying to drag me out of the car, but I was convinced that if I let go of the seat that they would pull me out and kill me, so I clung to the back of that seat for dear life. I got punched, kicked, and I had the entire top half of my clothes torn off from me until I was entirely naked from the waist up and they ripped my hair out in clumps. I was crying my eyes out in physical pain and shame, and I remember seeing a bunch of guys outside the car laughing. Then all of a sudden, the guy whose child had been christened rushed to the car and dragged these girls off me. The taxi driver and my friends were then let back into the car and he dropped us home.

When we reached my house, we were greeted by my mother's smile. She was excited to hear how we had enjoyed ourselves as she knew the previous week was a bad one for me, but one look at me and her smile turned to sheer terror. I ran to her crying and I told her what had happened. My friends then left and my mother took me upstairs and started to take out what was left of the cornrow that was in my hair. I can't imagine how she must have felt to see her daughter that had recently been stabbed, now battered and bruised again for no reason whatsoever. All I know is that she made an appointment to see the local councillor of our area the next day, to try and see if we could get a move to London as she was worried for my safety and wanted to get me away from it all. I wasn't having any of it though, because despite the attempts on my life, I had finally met a boy that I believed I was in love with, and I wasn't ready to break up with him to move to London. So I begged my mother not to force me to go, and in the end she didn't. Again, the stresses of life were getting too much for me so my mother insisted that I go and stay with my God-mother in London for a few days. During this time I had my first out of body experience; which was very scary. I recall lying in bed half asleep, and then hearing a strange ringing noise, the next thing I remember is having a sense that I wasn't in my body and then looking down and seeing myself lying in the bed. I don't remember much else except that I then woke up out of my sleep and I was back in bed. I never mentioned this to anyone because I didn't want anybody to think that I was raving mad lunatic but it wasn't the last time it was going to happen. A month after, I ended up breaking up with my boyfriend as I became weary by his ex-girlfriend saying that he was cheating with her. By this time, I had had enough of hearing about it. So we parted ways, and I began to accept that a happy-ever-after was not soon coming. So I just continued on with my promiscuous lifestyle, not realizing that something life changing was just around the corner.

Chapter 4
SUFFERING IN SILENCE

I started college in September 2001 and I enjoyed my

course very much. I was studying Leisure and Tourism and I planned to be an air hostess once I had finished. I still had my job in McDonalds which I attended on my days off from college. Whilst working in McDonalds a guy by the name of Damon kept coming in and asking for my number so, in the end, I decided to give it to him as I felt that I had nothing to lose. One day Damon invited me around to his mother's house as it was his mother's birthday, and she was going out. We thought it would be a good time to be alone and get to know each other. Once I got there, his mother pretty much left the house straight away, and instead of "getting to know each other" like I thought we would, Damon led me up to his bedroom. We didn't end up using any contraception that night but Damon reassured me, that everything was okay – that I wouldn't get pregnant; and foolishly enough I believed him. It's strange because I knew that contraception protected me against diseases but I never thought about how it also protects from pregnancy. I honestly don't feel that I was made aware enough about contraception and pregnancy. That night was the first time we had slept together. I didn't think anything of it - until less than a month later when I missed my period did I honestly think about the consequences. I started to get worried so I made an appointment to go to the Brook Clinic to get tested. The nurse informed me that the result was negative. Deep down in my heart I knew I was pregnant. They say that a woman usually knows when she is with child. Even so, I left the Brook Clinic feeling partially reassured that at least the result said negative but I decided that if I still hadn't come on a week later I would go back to the Clinic, and get tested again. It was no surprise to me when my period still hadn't shown a week after the test – this was almost a week and a half past my due date, so I decided to go back to the Clinic, only this time with my friend Janet in tow. Only this time the results were different and I was told, there and then, that I was pregnant; 2 months after my 17th birthday! To say I was shocked is an understatement, but I was glad to finally know the truth. The pregnancy now being confirmed placed a huge burden on me. I never intended to keep my baby, the first thing I did was go to see my cousin Nyomi who got me some leaflets on abortions. I then contacted Damon to tell him the news and he was not happy. He called me every name under the sun then claimed the baby couldn't possibly be his as I had slept around. Then he said that I must get an abortion, and I told him that was what I planned to do anyway. Damon's words really hit me and I realised that he didn't have any respect for me whatsoever; but then again I didn't really respect myself much. I remember the day that I decided that I was going to keep my child, I went to my cousin Nyomi's house, and whilst sitting in her room deciding on where I was going to go for the procedure, something came over me and I just felt the overwhelming desire to keep my baby. I remember telling my cousin how I felt and her words were: *"If you want to keep your baby then keep your baby!"* I knew then that THAT was the right thing to do. I was worried about how I was going to tell my mother but I decided to leave that for a later date. I chose to drop out of College as I didn't want to be attending College with a big stomach. Thinking back now, I regret leaving as I know that I could have still gained my qualification whilst pregnant, but I didn't think that at the time. When I informed Damon that I had decided to keep my baby, all hell broke loose. He continued to claim that my baby wasn't his and that he had heard how I had slept around and that I was a slag (a promiscuous woman). Then, to make matters worse, he then insisted that I meet him and his cousin in town the next day so that they could escort me to the Brook Clinic for another pregnancy test, as he believed that I was lying. I met up with him and his cousin and I felt so intimidated walking to the Brook Clinic with them both walking behind me like prison security guards. We arrived at the Brook, and after another test, the nurse informed me yet again that I was pregnant. They frog marched me to the bus stop and then I went onto the bus and went home. Funnily enough, a couple of days later, I received a phone call from Damon's mum Christine, asking me if I was pregnant. I confirmed that I was, and she asked me if I had told my mother. I was afraid to, so she asked me if I would like her to do it, which I appreciated. So we agreed for her to tell my mother the next day. The next day, my cousin Nyomi and her mum were at my house and I was waiting on the call from Christine. I was so afraid of my mum's reaction but I knew that she had to know the truth. When Christine rang, my aunt answered the phone and started to inform my mother of what Christine was saying but as soon as my mum heard the words, **'Chantell.........pregnant'** she switched off and didn't want to hear anymore. She didn't even speak to me. Then as if right on cue, the front door knocked and it was Damon. By this time I didn't know what to do with myself; everything was out of my control. He came into the house and proceeded to tell my mother and aunt how unprepared he was for a baby, that I should have an abortion, and that the baby may not be his anyway. He was acting and babbling like a mad man whilst I just sat in silence not knowing what to do. My mum interjected, and said: *"If you want to keep your baby Chantell, I will be here to support you"*. That was all that I needed to hear, but obviously not what Damon wanted to hear. When I went into the kitchen to get a drink Damon followed me and said words that I will never forget; *"Chantell if you get rid of this baby I will pay you"*. I felt sick hearing those words, and I had already made up my mind that I wanted to keep my baby.

Damon left my house in a huff and I didn't hear from him for a few weeks.

During my first few months of pregnancy I was still suffering from OCD quite badly but it just became a part of my life, though I tried to control it. I was also getting more vivid dreams about God and the devil, but I just put it down to stress. The day came for the girl's court case for attacking me and biting me, as they were eventually now caught. When I arrived at court with my mother for the trial, my stomach was already beginning to show. The girl that had bit me came and sat right beside me with her friends. She started to taunt and sarcastically mock me by saying how glad she was that she wasn't pregnant, and how she hadn't got any *baggage* (talk about intimidation). Then I got called into a room by the officer who informed me that the case had been thrown out due to some minor errors. I was so upset about this as the girl that stabbed me had recently got off with that as well. She had claimed that she was making a sandwich then came outside and the knife "accidentally slipped" into my back. I left the court feeling let down by the authorities but I knew that I had to get on with my life.

I handed in my notice at McDonalds as I started to feel sick every time that I was in there, so I ended up getting a job in the chicken place not far from my mother's house. One day I was upstairs on the bus going to work, my stomach still relatively small. A group of guys came onto the bus, sat down behind me and tried to speak to me. I had had enough of men by then so I decided to ignore them. Then I heard one whisper to the other, *'just spit on her.'* Even though the guy didn't spit on me, I felt so degraded and worthless. *'Why were men treating me this way?'* I wondered to myself, as I got off the bus at the next stop and hurried to work. I gave my baby bump a rub, hopeful that one day life would be better for me and my child. I saved up every penny that I could so that I could get essential baby items, I was really looking forward to having someone to love and that would love me back unconditionally. Damon contacted me every now and again to see how I was doing but he didn't help with buying anything. However, his mum Christine was a godsend. She accompanied me to both of my scans, and was also there for me whenever I needed support with anything. Then one day, when I was about 8 months pregnant, Damon decided to get with me for the sake of our baby.

On the 23rd July 2002 my beautiful bundle of joy was born, after 72 hours of slow labour. When I found out that she was a girl I was so overjoyed and decided to call her Siantae, as the name was similar to mine and with the hope that with the two of us sharing similar names, we would perhaps be really close. Siantae entered this world with my mum, her dad, his mum, my auntie Norma and 2 midwives by my side. Let's just say that this was a *very* eventful day and by the end of it I was exhausted. When everyone left I decided to feed Siantae, and then just simply rest with her for a while in my arms. Then the strangest thing happened to me. I must have drifted off to sleep as I felt myself leave my body. I remember being in a lonely dark place, it was cold and my whole body was tingling all over. I have felt loneliness in my time but I have never been as lonely as I felt in that place that night. I then subconsciously remembered that my baby was lying on the bed next to me in the hospital, and feeling an overwhelming feeling to go back to protect her so that she didn't fall off the bed. Then, the next thing I remember is waking up with Siantae still in my arms, so I quickly put her into her cot and then I went to sleep. Two days after having Siantae, I was sent home and I quickly got into the sleepless nights of bottle feeding every 2 hours, changing nappies and crying! Damon was there to help out and I must say that he did try his best to help me. Now, with having a baby to look after, I felt like I had something special to do with my life. Siantae brought me joy and happiness and I felt loved for the first time. I also received a house from the housing association for Siantae and me to move in to as a family. I didn't plan to move in straight away as I knew that I wanted to decorate and make it a home before leaving my mother's house. Damon continued to stay every other night with us at my mother's. I know that the LORD is protecting Siantae just as much as He's protecting me, as one day Siantae, Damon and I were in bed, and Siantae must have only been a few weeks old and we were all very tired. I don't remember falling asleep but what I do remember is the phone ringing at 3 am in the early hours of the morning. It was my mother who had stayed over at her friends that night. I asked her why she called so late and she strangely answered that she was just calling to check that we are all okay. I looked on the bed next to me and to my horror Damon was asleep with his whole body completely covering Siantae. I quickly shook him awake and when I checked Siantae, she was fine. I wholeheartedly believe that the LORD allowed my mother to call at just that precise time in order to protect Siantae from being smothered. Thank you Jesus! During this time I was still getting weird dreams. One night I went to bed feeling a little strange and wondering why I felt so scared to fall asleep. When I did fall asleep I had a dream that I will never forget. In my dream, I was in my new house and was standing in the room which was to be Siantae's, and with my arms outstretched like Jesus on the cross. Then I felt two invisible opposing forces pulling me from each side, but in the dream I knew that one was God, and the other was Satan. Then all of a sudden I remember being surrounded and covered by mud and looking upwards. I woke up out of my sleep sweating and feeling scared. I quickly fell back to sleep and my dream continued from where it left off. My whole body shot up out of the mud like a cannonball and ascended into a bright clear blue sky. Then I woke up uttering words that I will never ever forget: *"Thank You God for showing me the way, You gave me the chance to live another day".* I now believe that this was Gods way of telling me that He would soon be bringing me up out of a horrible pit, out of the miry clay.

"He lifted me out of the pit of despair, out of the mud and the mire. He set my feet on solid ground and steadied me as I walked along." (Psalm 40:2 NLT).

I felt a sense of peace and I knew that God was calling me. I soon realised that getting with Damon I was maybe one of the biggest mistakes I had in made my life. Don't get me wrong - Damon could be a lovely person when he wanted to, but when he smoked Cannabis he was a different person altogether. First it was the insults, him telling me that I wasn't a good mother, which made me feel worthless and insecure. Then after this episode, he verbally tormented me by telling me that he was cheating on me as I was rubbish, and not worth any attention from him. I didn't realise the first time Damon hit me that this would continue for as long as I stayed with him. Damon would beat me on a regular basis and I would do my best to hide my bruises so that no one knew what was going on at home. I was so embarrassed about what was happening to me, and I was scared to call the police because I was scared of what he might do to me.

Damon once beat me at his mother's house and his family called the police. Another time he chased me around his mother's house with a knife with only his brother protecting me behind the lounge door. I later dropped the charges as Damon managed to talk me out of it. The only time that I felt that I had a chance of escape was the many times that he ended up getting locked up for either selling drugs or attacking someone on the street. Damon called me every name under the sun and he didn't cease to remind me of how worthless and how no man would ever want me because every man has had me, and I'm nothing! I cried many nights lamenting how I had a baby for such a monster. I didn't tell people what was happening to me but I know that those closest to me knew that something was up with me. One day Damon attacked my sister, my best friend

Sara and me in my mother's house whilst my mother was on the other end of the phone and could hear us screaming. She called the police but by the time that they came, Damon had already left. I know that a lot of people reading this will probably wonder why I didn't just up and leave; but the problem with domestic violence is the perpetrator usually make's the victim feel at such an all-time worthless low, that till they feel that nobody else will want them. They cling to the hope that maybe if THEY do something different the abuser will change. I honestly felt like the reason he beat me was entirely my fault, and that I just had to adjust myself to make him love me more. I remember when Siantae was still very little, Damon punched me in the face in front of her, I knew that this was the last straw as he really scared Siantae, and I was worried of how this would affect her possibly in the future. So when he got locked up a couple of weeks later for ABH (Actual Bodily Harm) against someone, I knew in my heart that I would never get back with him and this time I meant it. The thing is Damon is my daughter's dad, and if I had thought that I had escaped so easily I couldn't have been more wrong.

Chapter 5
<u>WHEN ANYTHING GOES</u>

A week after my 18th birthday, I passed my driving test

(first time); I also finally finished the decorating and was able to move into our new home. Passing my driving test was a great achievement for me as I didn't want to be taking my newborn on the bus. Also, the fact that we had now moved into our own home was amazing. This should have boosted my self esteem but it was very low, and I began craving male attention once again to make me feel better about myself. I became as promiscuous as I was before I met Damon, and I felt worse about myself every day. Money was very tight for Siantae, and me. There were many times where I would have to starve just so that I could feed my baby. Many times, where I would lay on my bed with Siantae did I use only ordinary household candles bringing light into the dark cold room. We went through so much together. She was my best friend, and I was hers. I really struggled with money at the time, so a year later when a friend suggested that I get into lap dancing, I jumped at the chance. Making money whilst receiving male attention seemed like a great idea and I couldn't wait to start.

My first day at the club was not what I expected. The atmosphere was very dark and seedy but welcoming. There was a stage in the middle of the floor with a pole in the middle and I wondered how I was supposed to dance around it without making a fool of myself. The house madam – the lady that is supposed to look after the girls (lap dancers), told me the rules which seemed like easy work. I was expected to approach men that came in, pretend to be interested in whatever they had to say, and then ask them if they wanted a private dance. A private dance consisted of being in a cubicle whilst dancing and taking all of my clothes off for money but the men were not permitted to touch me. I thought to myself that should be easy, as I pretend to be interested in what men have to say every day, and I felt confident enough in my body to get naked for money. I left with £100 and I felt on top of the world. £100 for teasing a man, whilst he showered me with attention was easy money, and I soon got hooked on lap dancing. I quickly became the favourite girl in the club. Even though I received the attention *fix* that I so desperately craved, my hope in men was going downhill. How could I ever trust any man - when most of the men that came to watch me take off my clothes appeared to be well respected men; and 90% of them told me that they were married or in relationships? It hurt so much to see this as I began to think more and more that all men were the same, and that I would never settle down with a good man. There weren't any out there as far as I was concerned. I spent more time at the club than I did with my friends because I was hooked on the money and the attention; even though for some reason or the other, the money didn't last. I started lap dancing all over the country in places like London, Northampton, Nottingham and Cheltenham when the horse racing was on, as this was a really quick way to make a lot of money. A lot of the other dancers fell out with me, as I became one of the top earners in the club. Ironically, even with this extra money and male attention I would still go home and cry myself to sleep as I felt that there was something missing in my life and I didn't know what it was. Siantae would spend a lot of time with her Nanny Christine on weekends, whilst I took my clothes off for money. I deeply regret this now as I feel that I didn't spend as much time as I should with my daughter when she was a toddler. My need for attention seemed to overtake Siantae's maternal need for me. It would crush me to see other women in happy relationships, and I seriously wondered what was wrong with me and why men didn't want to stay with me. As far as I was concerned my earthly father didn't want me, my step-dad didn't want me, and now men out there didn't want me. I felt at an all time low, and I sadistically wanted other women to feel the pain that I felt of being broken. I remember one day sitting with a friend of mine who was married, and asking her how she had found a man to stay with her. I genuinely didn't know how to make a man stay with me and I wanted to know what I was doing different to anyone else, but at the same time I saw all men as cheats and didn't feel that any of them could be trusted. One night I was in West London staying with my cousin and a guy that I had given my number to a few months back called me. He asked me what I was up to and whether he could come and collect me, so I agreed that he could. When he arrived, I didn't recognise his face as the person that I had given my number to but he had come all of this way, so I decided to go with him anyway. After a long drive, he took me to a hotel in East London, and whilst in there he asked me if I would have sex with him. I didn't want to sleep with him as I didn't even recognise him but he stated that unless I slept with him, he wouldn't take me back to my cousin and that he would leave me stranded. I didn't know what to do as I had left my purse at my cousins and didn't have any credit on my phone. I reluctantly agreed to have sex with him as long as he had protection. During us having sex we somehow ended up in the bathroom. The next thing that I remember is the bathroom door slowly open and someone was watching us. I then realised that he must have set this whole thing up and called his friend to watch us. I was so shaken and scared; I told him that I wanted to stop. His friend then left and I quickly went into the bedroom and sat on the bed feeling degraded and ashamed. The guy then decided to call who I believed to be his girlfriend whilst I was sat there silently crying on the bed. He called to let her know that he was at his friend's house chilling playing computer games. I sat there in shock, naked on the bed whilst this guy lied to his girl about his whereabouts. He finally took me back to my cousins and I never saw or spoke to him ever again.

In July 2005, 2 months before my 21st birthday, I decided to treat myself to a holiday trip to 'Ayia Napa', in Cyprus with my friend Deena. A month before flying out, I had slept with a guy (only once) but then he didn't contact me again as I suppose he had got what he wanted easily. I didn't make men wait for my body; I gave it over easily as if it was some sort of free gift. Whilst in Ayia Napa, I was due on my period, but my due date came and went with no sign of my period. I was having too much fun in Ayia Napa partying every night, and shamelessly meeting up with guys to even care or think that I had missed my period; even though my stomach was looking a little swollen! I quickly pushed it to back of my mind and continued to drink heavily and party hard. I think that I was in denial! When we got back home, I took a pregnancy test which confirmed that I was pregnant! I didn't know what to do as I couldn't handle having another baby right now. I was messed up and having another new baby wouldn't make the situation any better. I also could not bear the thought of an abortion. Whilst I was contemplating what to do, my friend invited me to a birthday party a few days later, which was to be held at a bar in the City Centre. I decided to go to cheer myself up. That night in the club, the most unimaginable thing happened. I went to use the toilet as I felt a weird sensation in my lower stomach as if something was moving down. When I got to the toilet and pulled down my underwear, I saw the most horrific thing; what looked like a fleshy pink tiny fetus in my knickers! I reluctantly picked it up with a tiny piece of the toilet roll, quickly threw it in the toilet and flushed it. Then I cried! I knew exactly what it was. I cried and cried when the realisation that I had killed my own baby hit me. I had drunk so much alcohol in Ayia Napa, that I had numbed my insides to the point where I had a pain free miscarriage. Then I started bleeding. I cried for days but then I went back into denial and tried to completely forget about it; not realising that I would grieve for that lost baby years later.

About a month after the miscarriage, I had taken my

daughter to the city centre to buy her some trainers. As I looked around the sports shop, Siantae who was about 2 and a half by this point, decided to sit on the floor and proceed to play with her teddy bear. Within seconds of me turning my head to pick up a pair of trainers, Siantae got up and bolted for the door. I screamed her name as I chased her out of the shop, knowing that outside was a very busy road where buses continuously drove down at full speed. I screamed for my baby like I've never screamed before, but Siantae continued to run. As I got to the door, I saw Siantae running towards the road, I also saw a Double Decker bus driving at full speed toward where she was about to step out. I was screaming as I saw my daughters foot touch the road, and I knew that this was about to end in the most unimaginable way. Within a second of Siantae's feet touching the road, out of nowhere a lady grabbed Siantae and dragged her back onto the pavement. I ran up to them both crying, whilst also telling Siantae off for what she had just done. As I turned around to say thank you to the lady who had just saved my daughters life, she was nowhere to be seen. I asked the gentleman next to me if he had seen where she went but he said that he didn't see any lady. I now believe that God sent His personal ministering, and protective angel once again to protect my daughter.

I met Neil in the lap dancing club. Neil was a property developer in his 40's with 2 children living in a very nice town, in a very nice house. Neil showered me with gifts, took me to nice restaurants and took me on wonderful trips. Neil also had a wife! I felt on top of the world with Neil, and if I'm totally honest, I secretly wanted his wife to find out about us. The affair with Neil lasted about 4 months, and he started to make promises to me about leaving his wife which I must admit scared me as I was only 21. Whilst seeing Neil, I also got involved with and started sleeping with the DJ at the Lap Dancing Club, and on Christmas Eve, 2005, I slept with him. And, this continued a couple more times over the next few weeks. Early 2006, I found out that I was pregnant again. I was confident that it couldn't be Neil's, as he had previously told me that he couldn't have any more children, having had a vasectomy after his 2nd child. I told the DJ that I was pregnant, and he insisted that the baby wasn't his so I devised a plan to tell Neil that it was his anyway. Neil couldn't understand how this had happened, but he said that he was very happy. I told him that I didn't know what to do but he wanted me to keep the baby. Two weeks after telling Neil about the pregnancy, I received a phone call from him crying. So much so, that I couldn't make out what he was saying, but what I could hear felt like someone had just punched me in the stomach. He said that he couldn't have this baby, and that he couldn't see me anymore as he really loved his wife and didn't want to leave her. Once again I cried. Crying seemed to be my favourite hobby. I cried all the way to the Clinic to have an abortion. I was only 6 weeks pregnant so I was able to have the abortion by oral administration (a miscarriage – induced tablet). I thought that this would be an easier option as I didn't want to be put to sleep, and as strange as it may sound; I convinced myself that it wasn't as terrible as having a surgical abortion. I didn't tell anybody about any of the pregnancies, not even my best friend Sara - as I just felt ashamed and wanted to keep all of this to myself. So after taking the tablet I went home to miscarry in pain, alone, whilst plotting my revenge on Neil. As I knew the area where Neil lived, his surname and his wife's name, it didn't take me long to find his address on the internet search engine. I then decided to write a four page letter to his wife to tell her everything. I drafted a letter telling her everything that had happened, what Neil told me about planning to leave her, how he wasn't happy... everything. I even mentioned Neil's previous mistress before meeting me. Then I addressed it to her and sent it. To this day I don't know if she ever read it but I would love to let them both know how sorry I am for the part that I played in that affair. I was messed up and wanted others to hurt like I was hurting. I pray that God forgives me for that affair and hope that it didn't destroy their marriage. I was so broken during the time that Neil decided that he didn't want to be with me, that I just didn't care about myself anymore; not that I cared about myself much before that anyway. I remember one night after a night out, whilst sitting in my car outside a pizza shop; a guy approached me and asked me for my number. I was so desperate for someone to at least hold me, that the guy not only got my number that night but I also ended up staying with him at his flat and giving myself to him. I didn't care what happened to me, I was numb from all of the pain that I felt, but I know that God protected me through it all. Not long after this, Damon came out of prison and was continuing to bully me and make my life hell, so for the rest of 2006, I just continued to be miserable, dance, make money, see guys and feel pain more and more because of what my life had become. What happened to the fairytale wedding that I had planned as a little girl whilst playing with my Barbie dolls? What happened to my knight in shining armour that I saw as a child whilst watching the cartoons of Cinderella and Snow White? Would I ever be happy like the women I saw in films? Or was I destined for a life of unhappiness and darkness? Little did I know that in 2007, darkness was just about to get even darker!!!

Chapter 6
CURSED IN NEW YORK

In early July 2007, I had a trip planned for Siantae and I

to go and visit my dad for 3-and-a-half weeks in New York. Damon had just gotten locked up again for 6 years, and I just needed a break from everything that I was going through. I was looking forward to this trip as I really missed my dad. We had spoken a lot more recently, and I loved him dearly. I also wanted Siantae to see him as she hadn't seen him since just after she was born (she was now almost 5). Little did I know that the "Big Apple" of New York was going to be a life changing holiday for me, and not in a good way! Just writing what happened in New York feels weird as the whole trip was very surreal. We arrived in New York on the 2nd July 2007. My father took us to an 'Independence Party' in the park, which was so much fun. Siantae was really enjoying herself and I took her to the park on many occasions so that she could have her own fun whilst mingling with other children. Finally spending some proper time with my father was great, as we got to rebuild the relationship that was broken when I was young. The shopping was *out of this world*; I shopped till I dropped, and I really enjoyed myself, spending a lot of money in the process. That was until about 2 weeks into the trip when Siantae, my dad and I were coming back from Harlem. We walked past a large Latina lady near my father's house. She called me over and quickly asked me if I realised that Siantae's father had a girlfriend when he got with me. I thought to myself that this woman must be a psychic and I was intrigued about what else she may have to say, (Damon did tell me after I got with him that he had had a girlfriend when we started seeing each other but broke up with her after we had slept together). The lady then told me that his ex-girlfriend had put a curse on him to make him fall in love with her. The curse was supposed to work like this; from information from her mother who was a practicing witch, she would make a drink which she had concocted together. She would then say certain spells over the drink. Then Damon would have to drink this drink. After consuming the drink, once he slept with her, he would be madly in love and obsessed with her from there on. Unfortunately after drinking this drink, Damon left her house. The person that he slept with that day was me! The day Siantae was conceived! This may all sound strange but to me it made common sense. It made sense as to why Damon was obsessed with me, and wouldn't leave me alone and continued to harass me. I've since come to realise that with Psychics, their source of information is demonic. At this time I was naively vulnerable, and none the wiser. She told me that I had been suffering from stomach aches, and that was the curse inside me. I believed this as I had been suffering with stomach aches for a long time. She then told me to do something extraordinary, she told me to buy an egg from the shop, sleep with it next to my bed and then come and see her the next day, so as mad as it sounds I did. I awoke next to the egg the following day, and quickly went to see the mysterious lady. She told me in deep confidentiality informing me about how the curse worked for me, and that the consequences now is - whenever I get with a man, he will never stay, I will *never* keep a man; men will never want to stay with me - until this curse leaves. I felt that this was my answer! This *must* be the reason why a man has never stayed with me. This woman was feeding me information and I was *buying* it. She said that the only way this would end is when I get the curse lifted (delivered) out of me, and that's what the egg was for. She said that the curse will be transferred to the egg and that she will bury the remains of the egg, making me free from the curse. I took the egg out of my bag, and she then told me that I had to rub it over my body whilst chanting something after her. After doing this, she then said that the curse has been transferred and that I would see it when we break the egg. She told me to put my hand on the egg and then crush it, so I did. When I crushed the egg, I saw the most horrendous sight that will stick with me forever. I saw this big dirty black root in the centre of the egg. I screamed! She screamed! Then she said that it was now out of me. I have never felt so unusual. She asked me for money which I gave her – this amounted to about £50, and then she said that she will bury the egg, and the curse will be finally gone. The next few days were like a trance. I felt very strange as if there was a weird aura around me, and I was really scared. A week before I was due to come home, I called my mother and asked her if she could borrow me some money so that I could get a flight back home straight away, as I didn't want to be in New York any longer. So she did. When I came home, I felt a dark cloud over my life, I started to get suicidal thoughts and if I thought I had low self-esteem before, this was worse. I felt so low and depressed. I felt that if I ended it all, nobody would even notice, but then I felt like a coward because I was even scared to kill myself by suicide. I started to have weird spiritual encounters in my house and I felt like there was always something there watching me. I became more anxious than ever, I was still struggling with lust on a daily basis, my life just felt dark and I was still suffering with OCD quite badly. I was afraid of the dark, I would not sleep without the TV on but this had been the case for years. I could not sleep with the light off at all unless somebody was with me and even then I found it a struggle. There would be times where I would wake out of my sleep to a shadow entering or leaving my room. Things were quite bad in my life at this time.

I met Dean at a nightclub in London and he said that he wanted to be with me, so I thought maybe the lady was right and the curse was gone. I quickly fell in love (or I emotionally thought it was love) with Dean. I even toned down the lap dancing as well. I wanted to spend all of my time with him, and he made me feel different to the other guys. He knew that I used to dance but he didn't know that I still danced occasionally. I started to become less interested in dancing! Even the days when I was completely broke, I just didn't want to go. I didn't want to be there anymore. Little did I know that during this time, God was working on me and making me not like things that He didn't like! I also stumbled onto UCB Gospel on my TV, by what seemed to be by pure chance. Every time I got home from somewhere, I would switch the TV onto UCB Gospel and the songs of praise to God would make me cry. I didn't know why this Gospel music would make me so emotional, but I cried *every* time it was on. My relationship with Dean was okay; he spent nearly every weekend in Birmingham but for some reason I didn't see a connection with him and Siantae. This bugged me - as I felt that any man that I was with needed to get along with my daughter. I was also very insecure when it came to him. I accused him of cheating on me most of the time as I had seen texts in his phone to other women. I would even go onto his Myspace network, to look at what kind of women he had on there as friends, and every time I would come across someone that looked pretty, I would cry and wonder why I didn't look like her. I would also ask myself what he was doing with me when there was better out there. Looking on his Myspace and in his phone was like a ritual to me and I just could not stop myself. I also started feeling that if he ever left me then I would definitely end it all as I felt that I would never get a guy better than him, or a nice guy that wanted me. I was obsessed with him, and I would beg him not to cheat on me or ever leave me. There were even times where I would have a dream, whilst sleeping, that he was cheating on me and then I would call him first thing in the morning, saying that I knew he was cheating. He must have thought that I was raving mad when I said that I saw it all in my dream, but he wasn't the first guy that this had happened with. I was tormented and I was obsessed with the fact that men had and would always cheat on me. I didn't have any peace. I was obsessed with this guy especially because he said things to me that made me feel worth a little something. He would tell me that I was the first girl that he ever imagined would have his children, and that I was the first girl that he ever imagined marrying! Whilst with Dean, I also had an overwhelming feeling that if I just start to go church I will feel at home and everything will be complete. I felt this on a regular basis but simply chose to ignore it. I continued to live a life of insecurity and jealousy with Dean. I constantly checked his phone, constantly listened to the lies that he told me when I found something and constantly told myself how worthless I was.

In February 2008, Dean took me to Portugal for Valentine's Day, and we had a lovely romantic few days there. This was the first guy that I felt I could spend forever with, and I didn't know how I managed to get with him. I had such low thoughts of myself that I felt grateful to be with him, and didn't want to lose someone that I had eventually fallen in love with. However, while we were away, we had an argument and I remember shouting: *'I don't need you, when I get back home I'm*

going to church and I won't need you anymore!!!'
Now, I don't know where those words came from or why I
said them, but those words couldn't have been truer. A
month after coming back from Portugal, it was my cousin
Sherelle's birthday in London. I was very excited as I
hadn't seen her for a few weeks, and couldn't wait to get
dressed up and go out with her. Her friend had gotten us
all some discounted rooms in the Hilton Hotel as she
worked there, so that made it even more exciting. The
Friday came and I loaded up my car for the drive to
London, this was a journey that I had previously done
hundreds of times. I was so looking forward to the hour
drive, and being able to just chill and listen to music.
When I hit the M40 everything was normal, I was excited
not only to see my cousin but to also see Dean. The
motorway was clear and the drive was smooth. Then
suddenly it hit me! The only way I can explain it, is that it
was like something *jumped into my body*. One minute I'm
in the fast lane doing 80 miles per hour, and the next I
was hyperventilating and scared. I was on the M40
having a full blown panic attack! I hadn't had a proper
one in a long while. I don't even know what brought it on
or where it came from, but it was the most scary and

dangerous situation that I could ever imagine myself to be in. I managed to calm myself down enough to pull into the slow lane behind a slow moving lorry. I stayed behind that lorry all the way to London. Whilst in London, I told Dean what had happened and he reassured me that I would be okay, and that he would come back to Birmingham with me on the Sunday so I didn't have to drive back alone. He made me feel very special. After all the partying on the weekend, Dean and I drove back to Birmingham. The journey was fine as I had him to speak to for comfort. The next day, on Bank Holiday Monday, Dean caught his train home. I would never have anticipated at that moment, that I was about to let him go, as I was about to find a greater Love.

CHAPTER 7

NEEDLE IN A HAYSTACK, THE LOST SHEEP

They say that, "when you least expect it that's when

true love finds you", and this couldn't have been more

true. On Saturday 29th, March 2008, I was desperate for

some money as I was struggling financially since I was

not dancing as often as I was before. I knew I had to go

to the Strip Club to work, as it was a certainty that I

wouldn't be leaving Spearmint Rhino with less than £300

that night. I had joined Spearmint Rhino a few months

previously as it was a place to make more money than

where I was before. I reluctantly went to work and whilst

there (*even though I was making some very good money*

that night), I couldn't shake off the feeling that I *had* to go

to church the next morning. At about 4 am, I asked the

manager if I could leave early as I wasn't due to finish for

another hour. He asked me why I wanted to leave early

as I was making good money, and I told him that it was

because I had to attend church when I woke up. Upon

hearing this, my manager and one of the bouncers burst out laughing, and my manager said that if I went to church I would set on fire. I shrugged off his sarcastic comments. Little did they or I realise, that would be the last time I would ever strip again.

I woke up relatively early on Sunday 30th March, and I called my mother's friend, Selena as I knew that she attended church. When I told her that I wanted to come to church that morning, she was encouraging and told me to meet her there at 11:30 am, in the morning. When I got to church, Selena introduced me to other members of the mixed congregation. It was a small congregation and everybody seemed very friendly and made me feel welcome. When it came to everybody singing and worshipping God, I felt very emotional and 'touched' by the words: just like how UCB Gospel on my TV had made me feel. That day there was a guest speaker and I vaguely remember her speaking about how we have to get on track with our lives, as God has called us to do great things. I considered my past and thought that God couldn't possibly have called me for anything as I had done many bad things in my life, and hurt so many people. There is a parable in the Holy Bible, where a shepherd leaves his flock of ninety-nine sheep in order to find the one, which is lost. It signifies Jesus Christ's attitude towards us as lost sinners. I was that lost Sheep!

So he told them this parable: "What man of you, having a hundred sheep, if he has lost one of them, does not leave the ninety-nine in the open country, and go after the one that is lost, until he finds it? And when he has found it, he lays it on his shoulders, rejoicing. And when he comes home, he calls together his friends and his neighbors, saying to them, 'Rejoice with me, for I have found my sheep that was lost.' Just so, I tell you, there will be more joy in heaven over one sinner who repents than over ninety-nine righteous persons who need no repentance

– (Luke 15:3-7)

At the end of her teaching, I remembered the lady saying: 'that God loved us', (notably I didn't think this was possible for me), and that if there was anybody in the church that didn't know God, that we should put our hands in the air if we wanted to become *'Born Again'*.

Now I had no idea what this religious terminology meant, being *'Born Again.'*. And, neither do I remember consciously putting my hand up in the air, but for some reason my hand went boldly up in the air, and the guest speaker called me forward to say the prayer for salvation over me and for me. I was told to recite, the prayer after her, and as I opened my mouth and spoke the first line: 'Dear LORD Jesus', a rush of emotion came over me, and I suddenly burst out crying uncontrollably. By God's grace, I managed to finish the prayer. During this prayer, I was told that I have to believe that Jesus Christ died for me to take away the penalty of my sins, and that God raised Him from the dead on the Third Day. I believed this wholeheartedly, and I confessed it. As I finished the prayer, the only way that I can describe the feeling that came over me - was a feeling that someone physically lifted a huge weight off my shoulders. It was surreal but I felt something lift off me. There and then I knew that my life would never ever be the same again! After church I was given my very own personal Holy Bible as a gift for me, and I distinctly remembered going to my grandmother's house and just sitting there smiling with unspeakable joy whilst telling my family that I had gotten saved, by surrendering my whole life to Jesus Christ. No one understood what this meant but I didn't care. All I knew was that I felt different; happier! When I got home, I called my other Nan (dad's mum) and informed her that I was now a Christian a new creature, a new creation – given a 'second chance' in Christ in God, and I remember her screaming praises to God and thanking Him for what He had done. She was extremely happy for me as she praised God for her answered prayer. She also said that now I was a Christian, I shouldn't be having sex anymore as it was classed as fornication. That I should now be saving my body until marriage. This was like a breath of fresh air to me. I knew I now had a 2nd chance at saving myself until marriage. So when I got off the phone to my Nan, I also immediately contacted Dean and told him about what had happened at church, and he said that he was really happy for me. When I told him that I wouldn't be able to have sex with him anymore, he didn't take that so well. He said that he wasn't having a girlfriend that he couldn't have sex with. I said to him that I could no longer be his girlfriend, and that was it! I had told the boy - that I thought that I was deeply in love with, that I couldn't be with him anymore because I had found God. For some reason it didn't affect me too much because now I felt that I had someone else that would love me unconditionally, and that was the LORD, HIMSELF!!!

I felt myself suddenly become unattached to Dean and instead attached to God. Not only did I let Dean go but I also made up my mind never to go back to stripping ever again. I felt strong at first, for I didn't know where all this strength came from but now I knew that it was God that gave me this strength. For His Word declares unto me personally, and to every believer in Christ Jesus that,

"I can do all things through Christ who strengthens me." **(PHILLIPIANS 4:13)**

Auntie Selena introduced me to some young Christian people, and I felt so very happy, I felt like I had found my place in life, with a fresh new sanctified and consecrated body. God had given me a fresh, new outlook on life. I felt that I could now do anything. My young friends showed me that I had stereotyped Christians in the past by thinking that being a Christian was for old and boring people, but I learned to understand that being a Christian was amazing and actually more fun then I ever thought it would be. My relationship grew with God in a way that I just cannot explain. I would be out with family or friends, and I would long to go home just so that I could read, pray and just be in Gods presence. Being in God's presence I felt that I was special, I felt that someone actually loved me, that I was wanted. God wanted me! It wasn't always easy though, I would have dreams nearly ever night that I was masturbating, and then I would wake up really tempted to do it but I knew deep down in the pit of my very soul, I had to be strong and fight off the demons of lust and masturbation. I also started to think about Dean, and wonder if I had done the right thing by breaking up with him. I hadn't spoken to him in 2 months, and I was starting to miss him. My prayers to God would be about Dean, begging God to bring him to church so that me and him could get married and be together, but I soon came to realise that God knows what we need in life; and when God says "no" to something, it's for our own good. We must continue to trust the LORD, even when He doesn't give us what we are desperately asking for. My non-Christian friends began to see from afar off huge changes in my character, in my personality, in my speech in my actions as I didn't go out clubbing anymore, as I continued daily to spend all my moments with God. I just simply wanted to be in His presence all the time, it's where I felt most secure and safe and accepted. Nearly every night, from the moment that I gave my life to the LORD, I would cry profusely. Not through sadness but through unspeakable joy. I was so overwhelmed with what the LORD had done, and how he had rescued me from my previous life. I couldn't understand why I felt so differently, happy and content! I was so thankful, I knew that I didn't deserve it, and it made me realise how much I was truly loved by God. It made me see that even though I had been deserted by so many people in the past, I was not deserted by Him. Some days though would come and go by, and still the lustful dreams re-surfaced on the back of my mind; sometimes becoming stronger than before, and I was starting to find it very difficult to not give in to the temptation. It's like these dreams were able to control my waking moments just like the dreams I would frequently have of Dean cheating in the past. The day I gave into lust and masturbated, I felt so ashamed and condemned. I felt that I was a failure and that God couldn't possibly love me now, and because of this feeling I started to hide away from God, just like the Holy Bible describes Adam and Eve's ordeal in the Book of Genesis – the Book of "First Beginnings", when they both committed sin in the Garden of Eden. Even though the masturbation happened one more time, I asked God for forgiveness whilst struggling to forgive myself. This led to a downward spiral in my life. For in the month of Spring, after a couple months of being saved, I met a guy at the bus stop and I felt lonely so I started to meet and stay at his house occasionally. I think deep down I was also really missing Dean, and was never without a man before. I always had someone to at least sleep with. Even though I didn't have sex with this guy; staying at his house was bad enough and I knew that it would eventually lead to sex if I carried on staying over. Then one night a friend invited me to his church in the evening, and the pastor was preaching in a way that really convicted me and made me feel like I needed to get this new guy out of my life. After the service I told the pastor what had been happening with this guy, and there and then I asked him to pray for me. After he prayed for me I went home and I humbly and sincerely repented; I told God how sorry I was and that I wanted Him to take this guy out of my life, and never allow him to contact me again. After that poignant emotional moment with God, I warmly felt free from this guy and just as I had asked for in prayer, he never ever contacted me ever again.

In the summer of 2008, a month before my 24th birthday, I decided to get water-baptised – 'fully immersed under the baptismal waters', and it was the most amazing feeling to see my family and close friends witness this transformation in me. I felt on top of the world and I felt an overwhelming sense of love from God. I knew that I did the right thing. The next day whilst in church, I received a prophecy from one of the members there, who while prophesying to me kept crying and telling me how much God loves me, and how He was pleased with what I did the day before. There were many other things that she told me regarding my family and the purpose in which God has called me for, in regards to helping, encouraging and supporting women to come to Him through my life story and testimony. I can confirm that most of what she said has actually happened. I love the way God honour's His word, and puts purpose into our lives. Even though it had been a few years since I lost a few babies of my own, I realised that I had put it to the back of my mind, as I had never grieved for them. After becoming a Christian I really don't know what happened but I started grieving these children in such a way that I couldn't stop thinking about them, every day. Feeling so guilty, I cried and cried because of what I had done and I asked God numerous times to forgive me, as I just didn't know how to forgive myself. I started to imagine the ages that they would have been at that time and wondered whether they would have been boys or girls. I cried for my babies and I felt an overwhelming feeling of emptiness. I asked God to take care of them in Heaven; and also asked Him to tell them that I was sorry for what I did. It was a hard time for me and it lasted months. One particular day I was prompted to pray, so I prayed and I asked God to help me to forgive myself for my past mistakes, and I can say today that even though I still cry for them, I know that I am forgiven by God and that gives me peace about it all. I can now forgive myself. They're with their Creator being taught the oracles of God in the Kingdom of Heaven, and, yes one day by God's great grace and great promise to His beloved children, I will see them all again!!!

Just after my birthday in September 2008, I was sitting

in my room and I had a thought to write down my feelings on paper. That was the day that I wrote my first poem which I called: *'Looking for Love'*. I never ever planned to share the poem that I wrote, but a couple of months later, my church where holding a special service where we could share something encouraging. Something inside of me told me to present the poem that I had written. I didn't realise that I would later on in my life subsequently write hundreds of poems from my heart, and travel to certain venues all over to perform them 'live'. A personal one that I penned was a poem to God at the beginning of my journey with Him, just after I wrote 'looking for love'. This poem was called 'Who am I?' I wrote it because I can honestly and unquestionably say that I didn't know who Chantell, truly was. I knew who Chantell was trying to be for 24 years, but did not know who the inner woman in me really was! I was always everything that everyone else wanted me to be, but I was never truly myself. I just didn't know myself - not even my favourite colour! I wrote the poem and I cried and cried, asking God who I was, and for God to show me who I am in His eyes. I wanted to see myself through the eyes of God to see what He loved about me; as I couldn't see anything within myself to love. I didn't realise that the answer was a process as I learnt over the years to get to know myself. Months after being saved, I took out the many piercing's that I had in my body. I had 5 piercing's excluding my ears, and I felt that it was only right to take these out. Not that anyone said that I should, but I knew that the reason I had these piercing's was to impress men when I used to strip, but now I only wanted to impress the LORD with my new lifestyle, and everything else. During this time, I was still afraid to sleep in the dark. One day after Bible Study at a friend's house, I decided that it was time that I got over this. I got into bed that night, and before I turned the light off I asked God to allow me to feel His peace. I remember that as soon as I turned the light off and got into bed the fear was overwhelming. I was so scared at the age of 24, to sleep without the light on! I remember laying there and saying to God: *"God I trust You! Please take this feeling away, as I believe that you have been protecting me, and will continue to protect me, no matter what"*. All of a sudden, a sense of peace came over me, and I felt like there was a cocoon all over me, from the crown of my head to the very soles of my feet in which no evil presence could penetrate. I had the most peaceful sleep that night, and I can honestly say that from that moment, I was never afraid of the dark again.

In early 2009, God was just showering me with numerous blessings. First, I got a job working as a Scheme Manager for the elderly. Even though it was agency work, I still saw it as a wonderful much needed blessing as I needed the money. I also started being asked to perform the poetry that I had written, at even more functions and it was a tremendous honour and blessing to me to share my life's experiences with others. I also remember when a mother at Siantae's ballet class had fallen out with me over something small and trivial, just after she had got us all tickets to go and see Disney on Ice in the Spring. The day I arrived at the NIA in Birmingham with Siantae, I sat down with the other mothers that she had gotten the tickets for. When she finally arrived, she said hello to everybody but completely ignored Siantae and me. I was so embarrassed, and I felt uncomfortable sitting with them. Suddenly, one of the guards came over to me and said that he has to pick 3 children out of the whole arena to go on the ice halfway through the show, and that Siantae is the first child that he would like to pick. He then continued to say to us that we would have to go and sit on the special seating right next to the ice. I knew immediately that God had set this up knowing how uncomfortable I felt. I could not stop smiling as I got up to take my new VIP seats near the ice. Another amazing personal blessing for me was when I got the car that I really wanted. My previous car had been taken by the bailiff's a year before, and auctioned off. Even though they took it, I had peace in my heart that the LORD would provide for me. Usually, when God takes something away from us, it gives Him a chance to give us something better. In August 2009, just after a youth event called 'Midnight Oil Summit', I saw a new shaped Astra model, and I recall saying to my friend Grace, that if I work hard for the next 7 months then by God's grace I would be able to afford that car. All I can say is a week later, after praying about the car for a day, Grace travelled down to Birmingham from Derby to visit me, and I was now driving an Astra that was only 2 years old! The day that I had prayed for the car, God allowed someone in my family to give me the money for it, and I bought it that week, cash. I remember the first time that I got in and drove it; I couldn't contain myself to stop screaming and thanking God for providing it for me. It was a very special moment. However, testing times were just around the corner.

Chapter 8
SEASON OF REBELLION

I can't remember why I began partying again, but

sometime in the month of September of 2009, I just felt a
massive compulsion to go out to a nightclub with my
friends. It was only meant to be an innocent night out, but
it was on one of these nights out that I again met up with
a guy that I used to sleep with. I don't quite remember
what happened, but next thing I know he was at my
house putting a condom on. I knew that what I was about
to do was very wrong. The last time that I had sex was
with Dean a week before I became a born again
Christian - which was 18 months previous, and I had
planned to now wait until I was official and legally
married, as I had slept with quite a few men in the past
and I felt that God was giving me a second chance to
wait. Even though I knew it was wrong I didn't feel strong
enough to say that it was not what I wanted to do, so I
succumbed and went ahead anyway. As soon as he

entered me I burst out crying uncontrollably. I had this overwhelming sense of guilt that I had just cheated on my true Love.........God, HIMSELF! Even though I cried like a baby, I didn't stop this man and I allowed him to carry on having sex with me. In fact, I became so hooked and caught up in this guy that for the next 2 months I allowed him to come see me, and have sex with me. I knew it was wrong but I felt powerless; as if that was all that I was worth. I remember going to church on one of the Sundays and feeling so guilty that I couldn't even lift my hands up to praise God. I felt like I was being a hypocrite, knowing that I was sleeping with someone, and knowing that it was wrong. The next thing I remember is a lady from church coming up to me, grabbing my arm and taking me outside. She said that she felt in her spirit that something was up with me, and as soon as she said that, I blurted out everything in confidence to her. She comforted me and told me that although it was wrong - as long as I am really sorry and repent, then God will forgive me. She prayed for me, and from that day, I cut off all contact with the guy and I started to focus back my attention on my love for God. During this time of seeking God, I continued to write more poems as I felt a sense of relief and healing as I wrote. I also started getting offers from different churches to come and share my poetry with them to inspire others. With a great sigh of relief, I knew that I was well and truly back on the right path and I felt deep in my heart how much God loved me, even though I was unfaithful to Him constantly. I realised that even though I doubted, and still had regular bouts of fear and anxiety, I knew that God really loved me and had a plan and purpose for my life. I felt that my life had such a bright future, and it was hard to imagine that it was as dark as it was before I came to know Christ. I started to attend Bible Studies at church and attend group meetings with some young people that Selena had introduced me to. I remember one day attending a seminar with a friend, and whilst there I listened to an author speak about a book which he wrote about business and how it became a bestseller. After the meeting I decided to ask the person what tips he had for me on writing a book. He asked me what kind of book (genre), that I would like to write - so I told him that it would be a book about my life, and how far the LORD has brought me. I didn't even get a chance to say anymore as his first words were 'Don't bother!' His words hit me like a ton of bricks, as I asked him, 'why?' He then stated that no one would want to read my book as people only want to read books that will help them. He wouldn't have understood that this book was to be written to help others to understand how powerful the LORD is. How He will help those that come to Him by offering them grace through salvation, and hopefully healing them from their spiritual, physical, mental, emotional and even financial wounds, as I truly believed God can do all things! I decided to keep that to myself. Even though I was moving on, deep down I still desperately wanted Dean to be a part of my life. I remember praying repeatedly that God would save Him that we could get married. I honestly thought in my heart that even though Dean was a cannabis smoking womaniser, I would not be able to get any man better than him. Even though I started to realise how much God loved me, it was still hard for me to look in the mirror and love myself (After being told how worthless you are in the past, sometimes its hard to believe otherwise). I truly felt that I wasn't worth anything, and that no man would ever want to stay with a woman like me. When I come to think of it now, it's so very sad that someone could have such low self-esteem, and hate themselves just because of what others have done and said to them. I remember many times trying to stare at my face in the mirror and having to look away because what I saw in the mirror, I hated. Before being a born again Christian, I recall one day just simply looking in the mirror and crying whilst saying the words: *'I hate myself, I hate myself'*. Whilst saying these words I was also planning to take my own life by suicide, but then backtracked because I was afraid of dying. I truly hated who I was. Even as I write this and share now all my life's experiences with you the reader of this book, the tears are falling like raindrops because I cannot believe that I felt that way about myself, when in fact I am a beautiful creation, blessed, protected, and truly loved by God Himself. In His Word, He describes us as being Fearfully & Wonderfully made in this beautiful psalm on the following pages.

Psalm 139

For the choir director: A psalm of David.

O LORD, you have examined my heart
  and know everything about me.
You know when I sit down or stand up.
  You know my thoughts even when I'm far away.
You see me when I travel
  and when I rest at home.
  You know everything I do.
You know what I am going to say
  even before I say it, LORD.
You go before me and follow me.
  You place your hand of blessing on my head.
Such knowledge is too wonderful for me,
  too great for me to understand!
I can never escape from your Spirit!
  I can never get away from your presence!
If I go up to heaven, you are there;
  if I go down to the grave, you are there.
If I ride the wings of the morning,
  if I dwell by the farthest oceans,
even there your hand will guide me,
  and your strength will support me

I could ask the darkness to hide me
  and the light around me to become night—
but even in darkness I cannot hide from you.
To you the night shines as bright as day.
  Darkness and light are the same to you.
You made all the delicate, inner parts of my body
  and knit me together in my mother's womb.
Thank you for making me so wonderfully complex!
  Your workmanship is marvellous—how well I know
it.
You watched me as I was being formed in utter
seclusion,
  as I was woven together in the dark of the womb.
You saw me before I was born.
  Every day of my life was recorded in your book.
Every moment was laid out
  before a single day had passed.
How precious are your thoughts about me, O God.
  They cannot be numbered!
I can't even count them;
  they outnumber the grains of sand!
And when I wake up,
  you are still with me!
O God, if only you would destroy the wicked!
  Get out of my life, you murderers!
They blaspheme you;
  your enemies misuse your name.

O LORD, shouldn't I hate those who hate you?
Shouldn't I despise those who oppose you?
Yes, I hate them with total hatred,
  for your enemies are my enemies.
Search me, O God, and know my heart;
  test me and know my anxious thoughts.
Point out anything in me that offends you,
  and lead me along the path of everlasting life.
(Psalm 139:14 NLT).

I understand now that I am loved and I am worth so

much to the LORD, and I also knew I was forgiven by my

Father in Heaven. *What is Forgiveness is like....?*

It is like moving home into a bright, fresh, brand new
house, and you don't go back to try and redecorate the
old house you have just moved from to make it look
better. You no longer own that old house. You have left
that place behind - and it's no longer yours! So any
decorating work that now needs to be done should be
done in the new house - the place where you are now!!!

Each day we live now, there will be sins in our lives for
which we need forgiveness - and that is given. That's the

end of it. There's no going back over yesterday's sins. Besides, there is no time to dwell in the past, for so much need's to be done in the present! God loves you now, as you are now, and Jesus Christ died for you as you are now. *"While we were still sinners, Christ died for us".* (ROMANS 5:8).

That means you reading this book today can be forgiven, healed and delivered the moment you accept Jesus Christ's death for yourself! In the (**Gospel** of **John chapter 8, verses 1-11**), we have one of the funniest stories found in the Holy Bible. The scenario is this: A woman is brought to the Master - Jesus Christ of Nazareth – for this woman was caught in the very act of adultery. This lady, this woman, plied her trade as a prostitute and was captured red-handed by her men accusers and they said to Jesus: *"Master, this woman was taken in adultery, in the very act. Now Moses in the law commanded us, that such should be stoned: but what sayest thou?"*

These same men must have been in the same room.

They must have been spectators, because you and I both know it takes two or more people to commit an act of adultery! Just like these men who made the accusations to the Master - Jesus Christ, concerning this woman caught in the act of adultery, they didn't know everything and what we don't know changes our agenda. These accusers most of them carrying large stones were not aware that Heaven was recording their every word they told Jesus; that the woman had been caught in the very act of adultery and the Law of Moses insists an adulteress must be stoned to death. Jesus Christ heard her accusers and began writing something on the ground. Maybe He was writing the words 'FORGIVENESS' or 'HYPOCRITES', whatever He wrote must have inspired Him to stand up and confront the woman's accusers with these powerful words from the same **chapter 8 of the Book of John's Gospel***: "He that is without sin among you, let him first cast a stone at her!"*

Jesus Christ of Nazareth having stepped in to repair the

vandalised life of this adulteress woman stooped down to write something on the ground again to wait for their answer. It wasn't long after all these men searched their own consciences and found they were all a bunch of lying hypocrites. They had all committed a sin; and probably the majority of them were also carrying the spirit of un-forgiveness as well, because every one of them that was present, carrying large rocks and stones to stone the woman began to throw them down and quickly leave the scene. They dropped their stones. My friend reading this book now, I don't know the stone or rock you're carrying against your brother or sister who has offended you today but I encourage you to drop them today. Because of the seriousness of this particular case (and any case for that matter), you need Jesus Christ to handle the outcome, for He is my Judge and he is your Judge and He wants us all to drop them stones. May Jesus Christ give you the grace to do it and do it quickly in His forgiving name I pray, AMEN!!!

The only reason why I can hold a Holy Bible in my hand today and call myself a Christian, a woman of God, a daughter of Zion, is because I have been forgiven by His amazing grace and His unconditional 'agape' love, that keeps no record of wrong doings, casts away all fear and covers a multitude of sins - that's what His great love does. Therefore, with boldness I can shout it from the roof-tops and in the towns, cities and nations of this world, I Chantell Leonie Hayles, I am a brand new creation in Christ Jesus, old things have passed away and behold all things are brand new. Once again because of the seriousness of this particular woman's case, Jesus Christ stepped in. For this reason only He came down from Heaven as the Living Word and the Word became flesh in order to complete the great miraculous work of salvation in our lives for His Father. The only reason we as Christians can approach the throne room of grace and mercy is because we have been forgiven. - Thank you Jesus! AMEN!!!

Even though I was worth so much to the LORD, (just like that adulteress woman I mentioned in the previous pages). Other Christians would NOT have the same grace and love toward me. One day, I was introduced to a group of ladies from Wolverhampton who I really liked and got along with. This was a huge thing for me as most of my life was spent with other girls hating, stabbing, or attacking me. I really had a lot of love for these girls so didn't hesitate when they invited me on a ladies holiday to Benidorm, Spain for a few days. Whilst there, they introduced me to a girl who wasn't a Christian but she was a very good friend of theirs. I got speaking to this girl and sharing my past with her. We really gelled and she shared a lot about a guy that she was in love with, but told me that he was a player and that he had many children with many different women. I advised her, (the best that I could), and really tried to support her, as she seemed distressed about it all. I even encouraged her to try to pray and give it all to the LORD Jesus Christ, as He had helped me with my own personal issues. When we got back to England, this particular girl invited me to her birthday meal along with her other friends that I knew. At this meal, the male person that she had been discussing in private with me in Benidorm suddenly turned up unannounced at her table. I was in total shock; my nerves were tingling, my stomach tightening by every second because I now realised that it was a guy that I had slept with when I was about 16 years of age! I became very uncomfortable, so I quickly called the other girls outside for a chat. Whilst outside I told them that I knew this boy from my former life-style, and that I wasn't sure what to do. They advised me to relax - that they would sort it all out. A few weeks later, I saw them all at a Christian Conference and wondered why this particular girl didn't speak to me. I then asked the other girls if they had told her what I had said. They confirmed to me that they had, and that this guy mentioned to them that I had a bad name and bad reputation, and that I was a slag and had slept with a lot of guys. After that, none of them spoke to me ever again. I was really hurt by it all as I thought that they were my friends, and I was so disappointed to see Christian friends turn on me for something that I had done way before they knew or met me, but I wasn't surprised as this had always been my experience with girls. This could have really made me think otherwise about being a Christian, but I knew that the LORD is good, and that my Christianity is based on my personal daily relationship with Him, and not others who choose not to accept me. I had a past, which the LORD gloriously redeemed, and if people chose not to speak to me because of my past then they weren't worthy of being called my friends anyway because the Holy Bible says in the (Book of Proverbs 17:17 NLT),

"A   friend   is   always   loyal, and a brother is born to help in time of need!"

Not only did these girls reject me but I also noticed rejection from friends that I used to party with in my past. As I got more and more close to God, our relationships fizzled out as we no longer had much in common. It was hurtful but at the same time I knew in my heart that where the LORD was taking me in my life, certain people couldn't go. Till up to this day, those girls haven't spoken to me. If I ever got the chance to speak to them again, or even if there was a chance that they would read this book, I would want to ask them one simple word: *"Why?"* Yes, I would confront them but not condemn them but I would most definitely ask them: *Why they decided to reject me based on my past? Why they would cut me off just because of someone's report about my life? Didn't they have a past? Didn't they have things that they were ashamed of? Were they all born without sin?* The LORD says in His infallible Word, these words found in the **(Gospel of John (the beloved of God), chapter 8, and verse 7)**: *"Let them that be without sin cast the first stone!"* (Italics mine).

I am a sinner – and you reading this book now – you're a sinner too – for we are all sinful people. So please don't judge me just because your sin might be completely differently to mine but we still sin, as no one, I repeat –

'NO ONE IS PERFECT!!!'

During the new Spring season of 2010, God did

another amazing thing for me. By now, I had been working for one specific agency just over a year now, and my little sister Cyan had just got a permanent job with Midland Heart Housing Association, as a Support Worker in a women's hostel. The day she started her new job, she boldly went up to her manager and said that she has a sister that would love to do something like this as well. The first unusual thing about this testimony is that the Manager said to my sister that she must give me an application form, and bring it straight back to him the next day. So I completed the form thinking how unusual it was for a manager to respond so quickly to something like this. On the Monday, approximately 4 days after handing the application back in, I received a call asking me to come for a job interview that coming Wednesday. I went for the interview and it went well. The second unusual thing about this testimony is that Friday, I received a call from the agency to say that they would be getting rid of me the following week so next week would be my last week. I didn't even fret; something inside of me knew that there was a blessing in all of this, and I felt that God had set up the interview for me knowing that the agency were about to get rid of me. So that weekend, I had an amazing feeling that I was about to get this job. On the Wednesday, exactly a week after the interview, I received a call from Midland Heart to say that they were offering me the job as a Tenancy Support Worker working with homeless people moving into new tenancies, and that they would like me to start on the following Monday. When I put the phone down, I screamed with happiness and praise, as I knew that God had set me up! So that Friday, I walked out of my agency job. A few days later on the Monday 1st March 2010, I walked straight into my permanent job with Midland Heart. The way it all worked out, I just knew that God had His way in all of this and I was so very grateful. I felt blessed, not realising that once again I was about embark on some more testing times of faith.

Chapter 9
WHEN THE PAST COMES TO HAUNT

There were times where every now and again I was

thinking, *"What if?"* and occasionally Dean would send

me a random text to remind me of his place in my heart.

All I yearned and longed for was a committed

relationship, were we both loved and supported each

other, and I wondered why that was so hard, so difficult. I

even started to believe that what the psychic woman had

said to me in New York was the truth, and that my

relationships were cursed. I tried to fight that thought, as I

know that the Holy Bible says that when we come to God

we are now a brand new creation, a brand new creature

in Christ, and that all old things have passed away and

all things are made new (**2 Corinthians 5:17).**

¹⁷ This means that anyone who belongs to Christ has become a new person. The old life is gone; a new life has begun!

Even though I tried to believe this, at the back of my mind I still also believed that what the lady had spoken to me in America, must still be true and that I was never going to settle down and be happy. Once again, I started clubbing, which seemed to be the norm for me whenever I felt lonely. Partying gave me a sense of acceptance, affirmation and attention. Even though it wasn't good attention, whenever I felt lonely, it's what I craved at that particular time when temptation kicked in and got the better of me. The clubbing became more and more often, even though I knew deep down in the soul of my being, that everything about it was wrong, but I felt like I couldn't stop as I didn't want to be at home alone. I noticed that whenever I went out clubbing, it would always open some sort of portal for the enemy to attack me again.

During these times, I would again experience weird

happenings whilst asleep in bed. An unknown force would attack me, so-much-so that I struggled to wake up from my slumber because some sinister devilish thing would hold me down. I also recollect one day while in this held down state, a voice spoke these words to me: *"Where's your Jesus now?"* As soon as I heard that voice, I started to call on the full deliverance name of Jesus Christ of Nazareth. This invisible evil force that had been assigned to attack me during my sleep and slumber periods quickly disappeared. That's the power of Almighty God in action when we call upon Him in times of trouble! Another time, as I lay in bed asleep, I remember the feeling of something getting in the bed next to me, and then quickly putting its arm around my neck. As I was asleep, I can only describe this by saying I looked up with spiritual eyes, and behold I saw a vision of my headboard attached to my bed being the gates of hell. Behind it were flames from a fire. I then started to call upon the name of Jesus, but in this spiritual dream state of mind it was a struggle to say any words. As soon as I shouted out the powerful name of **JESUS**, whatever it was that had its arm around my neck started to scream out in pain. It then suddenly let go, and disappeared. These strange goings on was normal for me, and it no longer scared me, as it was to me part of paying a price for being a Christian. I believed through my faith in Christ Jesus, that neither Satan (my real enemy) nor any of his demons could hurt me. I knew in my heart that all of this was a sly tactic of my enemy Satan, in order to try to put fear into my life. One day, through sheer loneliness, I got back in contact with Dean through the popular social network site, 'Facebook'. I now know at that time I was in a very vulnerable place as I hadn't been spending real quality time in communion with God, and I had let my guard down. Dean told me that he knew that he was the one for me, and somehow I fell for it and told him that we can get back together. That was one of my most hasty foolish decisions I made as a Christian! The same day that we decided to get back together, I told Dean that I urgently needed to see him. He told me that he was busy, and he would see if he was free on the weekend, but that was on the conditional promise I would have to be the one to visit him in London. At that point, I was willing to do anything just so I could spend some time with him. Yes, somehow he still had a firm hold on me. That week I could not stop calling him up and asking him if he was free but he wouldn't give me a straight answer until the Thursday evening, where he said that I could come down and spend the weekend with him. I felt like all my Christmas's had come all at once, and that the person that I had always loved would now be with me forever. I could not have been more wrong! I was so excited but deep down in my heart I knew that this wasn't right and definitely wasn't ordained by God. Even so, I didn't care. I just wanted Dean to love me again. On that Friday I dropped off Siantae to her Nan's, jumped in my car and sped off to London fighting my fear, and motorway anxiety; the determination to see him again overcame any fear that I had regarding motorways. It took me quite a while to get into London but when I saw him and looked into his eyes, I realised why I hadn't been able to forget about him after all these years. I just wanted to spend my life with him. All that mattered to me was that I had Dean back in my arms. So much so that I unfortunately compromised myself, and my Christian beliefs yet again, and I slept with him that very night, and the remainder of the weekend. As with my previous lover a year before, as soon as we started having sex I burst out crying. I believe that the reason why I burst out crying now was because deep down I knew it was wrong. I felt like I had let God and myself down badly, as I really wanted to wait until I was married. For my body was after becoming a Christian supposed to be a temple of the Holy Spirit, not something for someone to lust over when they're feeling horny or to mess about with. Other than what my conscience was shouting at me, the weekend was a nice weekend, and I left on Sunday feeling on top of the world - but there and then when I finally got back home again - something strange happened to me. All of the negative feelings that I had previously felt when I was with Dean many years back, now started to resurface their ugly head's again! In the first 2 days of leaving London, I started to begin to hate myself again; I started looking at myself as worthless and not being good enough for someone like Dean. I forgot everything that God had said or spoken about me, and instead I bought into the lie of the devil, that I was nothing and worthless. Due to these negative feelings, I was constantly calling Dean throughout the week asking when I could see him again. This time he was behaving differently; he told me that I need to stop calling him so much as it was stressing his head out as he said, I was constantly 'on his case'. It hurt so much to hear these words so I then texted him, asking why he was being this hurtful way. This was when he started to ignore me. Then I started to entertain in my mind a weird plan of action that suddenly came into my head. I planned that the next time that I see him, I was going to have sex with him and get pregnant; that way he could never leave me. This thought played on my mind for the next few days as I continued to call and text him without success. I was adamant that I was going to have his baby, and then at last we would never be apart again. I didn't believe that this could be the same person that had pursued me since we broke up in 2008 without giving up. I thought that maybe he was just having a bad week, but he started to become more and more harsher, and basically he told me in not so many words that I should *leave him alone*. Our relationship had lasted 1 whole week; I was heartbroken. I didn't think that this could really be happening to me. I didn't understand why he would pursue me, sleep with me, and then tell me to go away. Didn't he see that I had a heart that couldn't handle any more pain? Why would he do this to me? I now believed that God allowed him to act this way toward me because the LORD wanted to protect me, as He knew that Dean wasn't the one for me. I had a plan in my head but God knew that this plan would probably more than likely destroy me. The LORD took over and didn't allow my plan to come to pass. How grateful I am now for the LORD'S intervention at that time. On that note, I would like to say this: "If you ever want to make God laugh, then just simply tell Him your plans!!!"

From that moment onwards, I decided that I didn't want another man in my life to break my heart, as my heart just couldn't take any more pain. It really hurt me that Dean had pursued me for all these years, yet didn't actually want me - he just wanted to see what he could get from me. Or, maybe he did want me but God knew that he wasn't the one for me. Either way, Dean and I weren't supposed to be together, and I finally learned to accept it at that period of time. I decided to get back on track with God, and try to focus on getting myself back together. I also decided that no man was ever going to have my body again until I was married. It was at this point where I decided that I was worth more than sex, that my body was a temple of the Holy Spirit and precious to God. I knew that for any man to have my body, he would first have to make me his legal wife. I realised that I was not good at picking men, and hoped that one day the right one would come along. A year after this whole scenario with Dean, along came Richard. Richard was to teach me that for my life to change; my mind and my actions had to change first.

Chapter 10

THE END IS ONLY THE BEGINNING IN DISGUISE

Whenen Richard came into my life it was unexpected.

He added me on Facebook just after Dean and I had broken up, but he hardly ever spoke to me. The most that he would do would like a status text or a picture that I had uploaded; he was just simply in the background really as I didn't particularly notice him. A couple months's after adding me, he did send me an inbox message saying that I should add him to my blackberry messenger as I inspire him with my Godly statuses, so I did. We started to speak a little on blackberry and we started to get to know each other, but I didn't see him in any way more than a contact. I wasn't physically attracted to Richard; he was just a really lovely guy. As the months passed, Richard and I started speaking a lot but I still didn't see him as anything more than a social media friend at most. One day I was in London with my cousin and we were wondering what to do. As Richard lived in London, I messaged him to ask him what was going on. He told me that there was a Comedy Show on and that he would also meet us there with a couple of his friends. When we got to where the event was supposed to be, we found out that it wasn't on - so my cousin, her friend and I decided to go for a meal. I messaged Richard as he was on his way and he decided to meet us at the restaurant. Even though I wasn't yet physically attracted to him, I was a bit nervous as this would be the first ever time for us to meet. When he got to the restaurant, we all hit it off straight away and then we decided to go somewhere else for milkshakes. After that first meeting with Richard I started to become attracted to him, as he was such a genuine lovely person. A few months after meeting, I decided that I wanted to go and see my dad in New York. Another friend of mine had decided that she wanted to see her family in New York also. I don't remember what made me ask but I decided to ask Richard whether he wanted to come to New York. He decided that he would most definitely come along, so we decided to book our plane tickets. At the last minute my friend decided to pull out of coming. So in March

2011, I went to New York with Richard to see my dad, and also for Richard and I to bond. Once again it was lovely to spend time with my dad and for Richard and me to bond. He told me that he liked me and asked me to be his girlfriend. After coming back from New York, Richard and I became officially boyfriend and girlfriend. He was a gentleman that would do anything for me, and it was something that I just wasn't used to. He said that we could wait together until marriage before having sex. He was so respectful. As time went on, I realised that it wasn't Richard that I was attracted to, no! For me it was his good, respectful, charming, gentleman mannerisms of the way that he treated me. Subsequently, I felt bad and I considered whether-or-not I could really and truly marry someone that I wasn't physically attracted to. Even though I knew that I wasn't attracted to him, I wasn't going to leave him either. I started praying constantly to God, asking Him to help me to love Richard like I knew Richard loved me. I felt guilty as I knew I didn't have feelings for him, yet I stayed because I couldn't cope with being alone; not after meeting someone that truly loved and adored me. Months down the line, feeling very insecure, I started to accuse Richard of everything under the sun. Deep down I knew that he was a good decent man, but my insecurities got the better of me. I remember being a very irrational girlfriend to him, and making his life a misery as I couldn't understand why a man would love me when all other men didn't care about me. I was in a relationship with someone that loved me, yet I couldn't get my head around it. I had been hurt so many times in my past by men, that I was subconsciously pushing Richard to his limits just to see how much he could take, and to also test his genuine love for me. During all of this, Richard still stood strong and remained attached to me. He also promised me that he wasn't like the guys from my past, and gave me his solemn word that he would never leave me. Something in me wanted to believe him but another part of me resorted back to the negative thinking that all men leave. Confronted with the possibility of being once and for all happy, my disturbed frustrated mind was now getting in the way of this becoming a plain reality. Richard tried his best to help but it wasn't enough, as my mental state (especially my mind), needed to be sorted out first. On the outside people thought that we were a perfect loving and happy couple, but deep down our relationship was a mess. I battled with thoughts of not being attracted to him as well as thoughts of not wanting him to leave me. It was a catch 22 situation. In February 2012, almost a year of being together, we decided to attend a Conference for couples called the 'Colours of Love'. Pastor Gbenga and his wife Selone were hosting this Conference. It was a deep revelation, and we learnt so much but sadly it wasn't enough for me as one day, a few weeks after the Conference, Richard had a week away with his boys. He came back to a tirade of messages from me, and I guess that was the breaking point for him. He contacted my mother, and asked her to support me as he couldn't be with me anymore; then he finally broke up with me! I can't say that I took it well because I didn't. I know that I wasn't attracted to him but to be rejected by a man that said that he wouldn't leave me really took its toll on me. I did my best to get him back but he wasn't having any of it. Deep down I knew that God allowed him to leave my life, because I would never have made him happy as I wasn't truly happy with him. God had to allow him to leave me as He knew that I wasn't strong enough to leave him. Even though I knew that this was the case, it didn't make things any easier for me, and I really struggled to come to grips with the fact that I was alone again. What hurt me the most was that Siantae really liked Richard and that he was the first positive male role model that she had in her life - as her dad was still making things hard for us, having recently come out of jail after serving just half of his 6 year prison sentence. All I wanted was for Siantae to feel like part of a family, were she had a positive role model in her life. I was worried that she would turn out like I was as a teenager, and that had always been my biggest fear. After breaking up with Richard, it affected my relationship with the LORD for a few months. I felt let down by God, and didn't feel like He cared about me because He was allowing me to hurt again. I still attended church but I wasn't paying much attention in all honesty. A few months after Richard broke up with me, I was scheduled to speak at a Christian Women's retreat in Wales but I did not want to do it as I had recently come out of a relationship, and I had no idea what I was going to speak about. How was I going to encourage others when I desperately needed encouragement myself? How was I going to speak to women about how to move forward in relationships when I had recently been dumped, because I didn't know how to act? It was at this time where God really worked on my heart, and I knew that my current situation would be the foundation on which I would firmly stand, in order to help other women to not make the same mistakes as me. I continuously prayed and God continuously gave me clarification on what I would speak about.

I went to Wales in May 2012, and gave one the best speeches that I could on: *'insecurities affecting relationships, low self-esteem and what we need to do as women to help ourselves to not end up in the same rut repeatedly'*. After speaking, I had women twice my age approach me for advice and feedback on the subjects of *insecurities* and *low self-esteem*. It was at that very moment I knew that God could use my past to help others in their messy situations; as God always takes a mess to turn it into a message for His glory - just like He did to and for me!. I knew that nothing that I had been through had been in vain, as God is Sovereign and He knows the beginning to the end, and everything in between! I finally understood what my purpose was in life, and I knew that God was going to use it to help free others from broken, busted, and disgusted lives and draw them closer to Him. One night as I was lying in bed, the words 'slave mentality' came to mind. I lay there pondering its meaning. Then it was revealed to me that my mind was like that of a prisoner that has been incarcerated for a long period of time. Once freed, the prisoner has no idea how to cope with the outside world so will do anything possible in order to end up back in jail; as that is the place that they are used to, and the only place where they feel comfortable. Even though the prisoner knows he is not in a good place; it is the only place that he feels comfortable so he will do anything to stay there. God revealed to me that night, that I was that prisoner. I was a *slave* to my own selfish thoughts and attitudes until I came to Christ, and by His great supernatural divine power and great grace, He freed me from the prison tyranny of my own thoughts and actions and attitudes. Even when I was introduced to Richard, this was inevitably a glorious chance for me to live in freedom, but once again I was so used to being insecure and jealous, that it became comfortable for me. Even though I didn't have to live a life of insecurity and jealousy anymore, it was easier for me as it was what I was used to! This ultimately brought along the consequences of my selfish thoughts and actions resulting in a good man leaving me. While all of this was taking place in the battle ground of my mind, the LORD showed me that I had two choices. I could continue to live in prison and be a slave to the negative thoughts or choose to be set free in and by Him.

One day I was talking to a friend of mine who attended

the church named: 'Calvary Chapel London'. My friend told me that the church was a Bible Teaching church, and that it would really help me to grow in my faith. We decided to look online to see if there was a Calvary Chapel in Birmingham, there was thank God! So, I decided there and then that I would try and attend the church the coming weekend with Siantae. When I attended the church that Sunday, I felt at home. Everybody was welcoming and I loved the teaching of the Word of God. It was different to what I was used to, as my previous church was 'Pentecostal', and my previous Pastor was a preacher more than he was a teacher. Calvary Chapel is based on sound Biblical teaching, and I knew that I was in the right place. Months after I attended Calvary Chapel for the first time, our Pastor announced that we would be moving to a new building, which would belong to the church (as we were renting our current building) at the time. The entire congregation was happy that we would now finally have our own church building, as we could now finally attend sessions during the week and truly make it our church, home. My pastor announced that our new church building would be in a basement, which was once a nightclub. Ironically the day that we attended our first service at our new church it turned out to be the same place where I miscarried 7 years before, in the cubicle of the nightclub at my friend's birthday party. God had turned it around full circle. The place where I had witnessed the darkness of death would now be the place that brings the Light of life – into my life!!!

Chapter 11
<u>LOVE NEVER FAILS</u>

Summer 2013 was quite a strange summer for me, for

at the beginning of summer I unfortunately had to take out an injunction against my daughter's dad as he was still continuing to harass me by turning up at my workplace and home. In my heart I was scared of Damon because he was irrational, and I remember once saying to a friend that if I ever ended up murdered, he would be the perpetrator. Within 2 months of receiving the injunction, he blatantly breached it twice and was arrested, and locked up in prison for a few months. I was worried about what he may do to me when he came out but God continued to protect me, and take away all my fears. The court awarded an injunction that didn't have an end date. To me that was a blessing in itself, as Damon continued to harass me for the next few years in which case he was arrested, and locked up many times for doing so. During 2013, I was also having a few ups and downs in regards to where I was at with the LORD, and where He was taking me in my ministry. Lust and masturbation AGAIN continued to be a huge struggle. Every time that I gave in to this demon of self-gratification, I felt so guilty and condemned but then I would beg the LORD for His sweet forgiveness, and try again to abstain. This became a regular pattern, and I just didn't know how to stop myself from doing it. It was a struggle no matter how hard I tried. I hadn't shared any poetry or speeches since May 2012, and I just wasn't sure what the LORD had planned for me. I can honestly say that I was in a confused place; I wasn't sure what I planned to do with my life. God had constantly blessed my life over the previous few years but I had come to a standstill in regards to my future. In all this confusion, I now had started speaking to a new guy who lived in London, called Ishmael, who I met up with a couple of times. At first he showed his interest in me and told me that I was now his girlfriend, but then he started to speak to me disrespectfully - making me feel unloved and unwanted. He wasn't remotely interested in me, because he only showed me or gave me just a little bit of attention; enough to keep me there in this rather odd relationship. I didn't understand why he was playing games with me but this wasn't the situation that I wanted to be in. He was not nice at all. I believe that he was confused as he had a lot of things going on in his life. I don't think that he even knew himself what he really wanted! His peculiar ways of treating me finally got to me so badly that I felt like I would never ever meet anyone that cared about me like Richard did. During this emotionally distressing time, I regretfully even sent an email to Richard telling him that he was the only one for me. Thankfully, Richard never responded! One day in June 2013, I lay in bed on my pillow and cried profusely to God asking Him why this guy was treating me this way. I couldn't take it anymore and I honestly had had enough but couldn't find the strength once again to break free. As I lay soaking the sheets with my tears, I felt as if I could hear God say, 'Wait'. I decided to wait on the LORD, because I knew that He would deal with this situation for me as He had always done in the past. A few weeks after hearing the LORD say 'Wait', I was at church and my pastor taught about being chained to situations, and how we must go to the LORD in order to break free from them. When he spoke, it was as if I felt strength come from nowhere, and I knew exactly what I had to do. When the service finished, I could not get out of church quick enough. I contacted Ishmael and told him that it was over, that I didn't want him to try to talk me out of it as I had made up my mind. He even had the audacity to ask me why I was acting this way and said that we could work it out. I asked him to leave me alone and that my mind was made up. I never spoke to him again.

In August, I received a Facebook message from a friend called Errol stating that he would really like to come to church as he wanted to change his life. What I didn't mention previously was that Errol and I had history from when I was about 19 and he was 24. Errol and I used to sleep together all those years ago but it was only for a short while, then we just so happened to stop speaking. I hadn't seen Errol for almost 10 years. The way he came back into my life, was very strange in itself. In the winter of 2012, Errol was on his way to work from jail as he was serving a 3-and-a-half year sentence, and was in an open prison where he had an opportunity to leave, go to work, and then go back to jail. This was to get him prepared for living in the community again. One day on his way to work, he spotted me in the local train station, as I was ready to board my train to London. When he came over, I called him Carl and gave him a hug. Carl was the name that Errol had given to me all those years ago, so at this point I had no idea that Carl was actually a fake name. I spoke to him in the train station, and informed him that I was now a Christian and had completed changed my life around (He recently told me that at that point he decided not to ask for my telephone number as he could see that I was different and not like in any way I was or had been many years ago). What was also strange was that almost exactly a week later, I saw Errol again as I left a nightclub with my friends. From us not seeing each other for almost 10 years to then seeing each other twice in the same week was a big thing for Errol, so he decided at that point to ask for my number. I decided to give him my number, and he asked at that point if he could stay over at my place as he was on home leave for the weekend from jail. I informed him that I was no longer the girl that he used to know, and that he couldn't stay with me. He then went on to say that he wouldn't try anything – and that he just wanted to chill out with me. As a Christian, I know that it is wrong to be sleeping in a bed with the opposite sex as we set ourselves up for all sorts of temptations. If I'm honest, I was very lonely at that point and really felt that the comfort of Errol's arms would perhaps somehow make me feel better; so I allowed him to stay. As promised, Errol didn't try anything with me that night, and I thoroughly enjoyed his company. A week later, whilst he was on home leave from jail again, I invited him to the church that I previously attended. Errol enjoyed the service, and said that it made him feel good. After attending church together later on for no particular reason our friendship some how sort of fizzled out for almost a year. Errol told me that during that year, he came out of jail and partied constantly as he just wanted to get it all out of his system after serving almost 4 years inside prison. One day he felt that he wanted a change in his life, and it was at this point in his life in August 2013, that he was the one who contacted me asking if he could attend my church.

The day that Errol attended my church was a great day all round. He told me that he felt very welcome at Calvary Chapel, Birmingham and that he would also like to attend the week after. I was pleased for him as I could see that he had developed a hunger for the LORD. This attracted so much of me to him, as I knew quite a lot about living a worldly lifestyle, and I unquestionably had become pretty much an expert about the lifestyle that he was willing to give up in order to come to the LORD. Hitherto, I must include that after Richard and I separated, in my daily prayers to God, I had personally asked in my petitions, supplications and requests to the LORD, to give me someone that had been out in the world; realised that the world was not enough to satisfy the soul, and wholeheartedly turn away from the world and it's worldly pleasures, and sincerely seek and want a personal living and loving personal relationship with the LORD. I felt that I needed a man like this - as only a man like this would be able to understand my past former life. A week after Errol's first attendance at my church, He came to see me share poetry at an event there. This was a big moment for me, as I hadn't shared any material (that I had written), for a few years and I knew that I wouldn't be able to glorify the LORD, however I was very nervous. For the fact that Errol had made it to see me share my gifts, and my talents, was a big thing for me. He even brought his daughter along to this event. I now was hooked on Errol, and became really and truly deeply attracted to him.

A few days later, he took me for a birthday meal and it was at this point where I really felt that maybe he could be the One. During this time I constantly prayed to the LORD, that He wouldn't allow me to fall 'Head over Heels' in love with Errol if he wasn't the one for me. I was tired of being hurt, and I simply wasn't going to allow that to happen again. On the 15th September 2013, Errol spoke to me, and told me that he had feelings for me as he could see qualities in me that he had never seen in any other girl he previously dated. He said that he was attracted to the faith that I had in God, and that he had never met anyone like me before. He then asked me to be his girlfriend. I literally said yes straight away and felt happy that I finally had my *'bad boy turned good'*. From the moment that we got together, Errol and I became inseparable and I made sure that I told him that I didn't plan to be intimate with him as I wanted to wait until Marriage. Errol respected that wholeheartedly and promised to wait with me. This was a big thing for me because I knew the lifestyle that Errol had come from. I knew that he never had to 'wait' with a woman before. The fact that he chose to wait with me spoke volumes as I knew how hard that would be for him, yet he was dedicated to me enough to want to wait. He was such a blessing! I told Errol everything about my past including what I was like with men. He never judged me once. I thought that it would put him off me, but instead he was quick to remind me it was my past, and that I was no longer that person. There were many times when he just held me as I cried about feeling abandoned by my step dad. He didn't have to say anything, holding me was more than enough. He held me tight enough to allow God to mend my broken shattered pieces back together. By this time I had built up a proper fulfilling relationship with my dad in New York, and we had become closer but I still had no real explanation as to why my step dad left and it still affected me quite bad. It was very hard for Errol in the first year or two, because I found it difficult to trust him even though he never gave me a reason not to. I constantly went through his mobile phone looking for evidence to back my unhealthy thoughts. As far as I was concerned, all men were cheats and no man would ever stay with me. I never found anything but it didn't stop me from looking. Sometimes, I would look hoping to find something just to justify my actions. It's like I wanted to find something but at the same time I didn't because I just wanted to be happy. It was a catch 22 situation for a long while. I built up a wall around me in order to try and protect myself but instead I just allowed myself to be trapped behind the wall that I had built! I just couldn't take being hurt again, and I would do anything to ensure that. I do believe it's because I still didn't understand why I was abandoned by my father at a young age, so I expected it from Errol. One day, Errol insisted that I needed to contact my step dad to let him know how I really felt. The first thing I did was write a poem called: **'Daddy, why did you leave?'** and I sent it to him, then asking him to call me. When he called me, I was able to get a huge weight off my chest. I told him how I felt; and what the effect of him leaving had done to my sister and me. I explained how him not calling us for all those years deeply affected my sister and I, and how I don't think that I had truly recovered as I'm still allowing the pain to affect my relationships now. He tried to explain why he left but didn't really do a good job of it. He promised there and then that he would call every month, and try to rebuild the relationship. After that phone call he didn't stick to what he said he would do, but it was different this time; being able to tell him just how I really and truly felt on the phone that day gave me closure, and that's all that I needed.

As our first anniversary approached, (of Errol and me being together), I began to worry. I eagerly anticipated reaching the first year milestone with Errol; so when it came and went, I was overwhelmed. I could not understand how I had lasted a year in a relationship with a man. This was not the norm for me! My longest relationship was 11 months, and that was with Richard. Our relationship wasn't easy in its humble beginnings on either part but we both loved each other, and we genuinely wanted to make it work. I really struggled with adjusting to the fact that I had a man in my life that wasn't going to leave me. I just couldn't understand it, and constantly expected him to leave. Errol tells me now that at times when it got hard, and he felt like leaving, he would hear the LORD speaking to him in his ear, telling him to stay. He also explained to me one time that when he went to jail previously, he knew that he had to go in order to be taken away from the distractions in his life. And, whilst in jail he continued to turn to his Bible and start reading; there he told me he felt the presence of the LORD. He said that had he not been in jail, he believes that he would have still been out in the world, handling guns and drug dealing to this day. God had to take him away from everything in order to begin a good work in his life, so after finally coming out of prison incarceration and meeting me, he knew that he knew that I was the one. The first year and a half for us was hard, as we both tried to establish boundaries, (what we wouldn't stand for in our relationship), and just trying to work out how to last because we loved each other. During this time, a couple of guys that I had slept with in my past uncannily just happened to turn out to be guys that Errol knew one way or another. They didn't delay or waste any of there precious time in immediately telling Errol how they knew me. It was Errol's incredible wise response that made me realise his love for me. He told them that even though they knew me from my past, that's exactly what it was - my past! He further added: That I was a completely different woman now, and he doesn't want to hear anything more about it. When he told me how he responded I was amazed. No man had ever stuck up for me like this before. It was most definitely love.

On our 2nd anniversary, on the 15th of September 2015; exactly 2 years since Errol asked me to be his girlfriend, Errol took me to a really nice Thai restaurant not too far from my house. As we ate, Errol then got down on one knee, and pulled out a beautiful white gold diamond ring and asked me to be his beloved wife. This was one of the happiest days of my life; and I said "yes" straight away. I could not believe that someone wanted to marry me, Chantell Leonie Douglas - the girl that men used and left, the promiscuous girl with the shameful past, the girl that no man ever wanted to stay with. Yet, Errol wanted me to be his wife forever! I knew that God was so involved with this relationship. I knew from the moment that he came back into my life. I just knew because when Errol and I first met, I was hard work and untrustworthy yet at this point having let my guard down, I was now able to be fully open and honest with him. Errol's love for me had broken down the walls that I had built to protect myself. Errol unquestionably loved me this I knew deep down in the very pit of my soul. I knew that his love for me is only a small representation of God's awesome love for me, and all His beloved children here on planet earth regardless of the colour of your skin or age group or social class or ethnicity. God loves me, with all of His heart, mind and Spirit, and has continuously been there and protected me all of my life. The LORD had changed my life in these 7 years as a Christian, and I knew that it would only get better!!!

Chapter 12

WHEN MY MESS

BECAME A MESSAGE

A month after being engaged, in the midst of wedding

planning I was asked to share poetry at an event called 'The Upper Room' in Wolverhampton. I attended it with some family and friends, and had written down the poem which I was going to share. My only intention was to share the one poem and that was it, but the LORD had other plans. I didn't realise at the time that attending this event would be such a life changer for me in regards to my ministry and purpose in the LORD. As I sat there riddled with nerves waiting for my turn to share, a guy stood up to share his testimony and it was really emotional. Then a lady stood up to share her testimony which was equally as touching. At this point I felt not only to share my poem but that I should also share my testimony; and not only my testimony but parts of my testimony that I had never shared before, like the lap dancing and the promiscuous lifestyle. I wasn't sure if this feeling was from God or just a thought in my head so I decided to ignore it. Less than 10 seconds later, my friend looked over at me and said: *"You need to tell them your testimony Chan, all of it!"* I knew then that the LORD had clearly spoken, as I stood up to share my testimony and then to recite my poem afterwards. Now was the time God wanted me to become transparent to the very people that the LORD was using me to draw to Him. As I stood up, my nerves disappeared and I felt the peace of God overwhelm me. I knew that this was the right thing to do! I shared my testimony that evening and it was liberating. The things that I was most ashamed of were now in the open, and no one judged me! Many people thanked me afterwards, saying that they now know that the LORD Jesus Christ can change lives. It didn't just stop there! The day after I shared my testimony at the event, I decided to be even more transparent and share the video of it with the world-wide public at large on Facebook. I was so nervous, wondering what people would think of me. It's one thing to share it in a room with hundreds of people, but to share it on such a public platform as Facebook is another completely different level. I wondered if people would look down on me. I wondered if Christian friends would disown me like the girls that I went to Benidorm with. I was scared of what would happen, but I knew that I wasn't doing this for myself; I was doing this because I knew that the LORD had called me to do it in order to show how Powerful He truly is. I knew that the LORD wanted to use my life to inspire and encourage others to show people that their lives can change only if they surrender their heart and give it to Him. The Holy Bible says: *"That there is therefore now no condemnation in Christ Jesus"* (Romans 8:1), so I shared the post of Facebook! I wasn't prepared for all of the encouragement that I received. I was so overwhelmed to see how many people were inspired by my life-changing journey and testimonies. I started instantly receiving Facebook inbox messages from women that weren't even my friends on Facebook asking for advice, and stating how my story had inspired them. I received messages off people asking if they could use my video to show the youth that they work with in their various locations. I also received messages off people stating that my story gave them hope. I honestly didn't expect all the love that I received, but I knew that all this was ordained by God. I knew that the purpose which I was told when I first became a Christian; what God had called me for, was actually taking place right in front of my eyes. My family was the only ones that weren't initially happy with me uploading my video as they are very private. At first my aunts and then my mum called, telling me that I must take the video off Facebook at once! They didn't understand that I have a calling that requires me to be transparent. After explaining to my mum and aunt about what the LORD had done in my life and how I believe that He is going to use my past to help others, they finally understood. Then when I showed my mum the actual video, she said that she was very proud of me and knew that this was God ordained!

A couple of days after uploading the video, I received

a message from Pastor Gbenga. This same pastor hosted the 'Colours of Love Conference' that I had attended back in 2012 with Richard a few weeks before we had broken up. Pastor Gbenga stated that he had watched my testimony, and that he would like me to come to London to be interviewed by him and to share my testimony with his church. I was excited as I knew that this was another opportunity to bring hope to more people and share with them the goodness of the LORD in the land of the living, so on Sunday 6th of December, 2015 I attended the 'Rock Church' in London. Pastor Gbenga interviewed me, asked various questions about my past, and really encouraged me in regards to my walk. This was recorded and uploaded to YouTube, and once again I was inundated with inbox messages from ladies asking for advice. All of these ladies that in-boxed me, I graciously pointed them in the direction of Jesus Christ. I let them know that the LORD Jesus Christ died for our sins, and that all we must do was believe and trust in Him to receive salvation for our souls. Salvation is the first step, and then comes transformation. He transformed me from the inside out, glory Hallelujah, AMEN!!!

In the Spring of 2016, I watched as my Fiancé Errol

made a declaration to the world that he chose Jesus by getting water-baptised by full immersion under the waters. I was so proud of him, and how far he had come in his Christian walk. I also got to see many times, how the LORD was bestowing miraculous blessings upon him in regards to his job. God was really blessing us individually and corporately, and I was so eternally grateful. Our Wedding planning wasn't easy as our initial date was set for the 17th of September, almost a year to the day that we got engaged. We chose this date because on the 15th of September 2013, we became boyfriend & girlfriend. Then on 15th September 2015, we got engaged so we wanted our wedding date to be the closest Saturday to the 15th of September. As Errol and I busied ourselves with wedding planning, I still had my struggles in regards to anxiety but the LORD brought me through it. One day, I was driving my car and I had a panic attack (I hadn't had a panic attack for years by this point). Then I started having panic attacks many times throughout the day. It got so bad that I couldn't get in my car and I couldn't even go to work. I had to stay at my mother's house so that she could look after me, as I was too afraid to stay at home alone whilst Siantae was at school. Everyday for the next 2 weeks I would have a panic attack, and I had no idea why? One day, I decided to call my nanny Hazel (on my dad's side of the family) as I knew that she was someone that loved to pray and I thought to myself that if anyone can help me get through this situation it is her. I felt this, as I didn't have any strength to pray myself. It sounds bad but I just couldn't find the strength to talk to the LORD whilst going through this dark time. Everything felt surreal, and I didn't feel like I was myself. I felt alone even though I had my family around me. My Nan came around one day with her friends from church and they prayed for me. The power that I felt in the room that day was amazing, and I knew that something was lifting off and out of me. I felt more peaceful inside. Less than a week after my Nan prayed, I was able to go back home and the panic attacks lessened. The day I was to return back to work was tough as I hadn't been in my car for almost 3 weeks. I knew it was time to stop avoiding it; as if I continued I wouldn't be able to go back to work. I remember getting into my car and reading God's Word. The Scripture that I clung on to was from the New Testament Book of Philippians Chapter 4, verses 6-7: ***"Be anxious for nothing, but in everything by prayer and supplication with thanksgiving let your requests be made known to God. And the peace of God, which surpasses all comprehension, will guard your hearts and your minds in Christ Jesus"***.

I told God that I believed that His Word was true so He has to honour my request, and take away all my fears. I drove to work in peaceful tranquility! As I got nearer to the City Centre, I could feel the adrenaline rising in my body and I knew another panic attack was imminent. As I sat there in my car at the traffic lights, I silently asked God to help me. I then looked up to see a bus in front of me. On the back of the bus was an advert saying **'TryPraying.Com'** I knew then that my LORD, my Shepherd was with me. From that moment I knew that I could trust in the LORD to be with me at all times.

Errol Hayles and I got married on the 17th of September, 2016 – praise God!!!

Our day was beautiful and everything that I had expected it to be. We got married in a beautiful church in Birmingham, and our reception was held at a golf course not far from home. All of our family and close friends were there to witness us exchanging our vows. Our main guest was the Triune God - God the Father, God the Son and God the Holy Spirit, and I knew that He had orchestrated everything to lead up to this amazing moment. After our reception we flew straight to Jamaica for our honeymoon for 2 weeks, and had a wonderful time. My love for Errol grew more and more for him the moment that I became his beloved wife, and I am so honoured and blessed to have him. Marriage life has its ups and downs, but I can honestly say that if God is the centre of the marriage, it will work! Not only does Errol love me but he also treats Siantae like his own biological daughter. Siantae doesn't have a good relationship with her dad and he continues to try to harass us even though an injunction was taken out on him in 2013. He's breached the injunction 4 times, and has been locked up a couple of times because of this. In the midst of it all, the LORD is still good and constantly protects, cares and provides for us. We couldn't have anticipated that all of our lives would be at a huge risk on a family holiday less than a year later.

In August 2017, a month before our 1st year wedding

anniversary, Errol, our children (consisting of Siantae and Errol's 3 children from previous relationships), my mother, sister, nephew, cousin and our friends went on an 18 person family holiday to Santa Susanna near Barcelona in Spain. On Thursday 17th of August we decided that we would get the train, and do a family trip to the Las Ramblas strip in Barcelona. I wasn't sure about going on this particular day but this was the day that everyone else wanted to travel on. When we reached the Las Ramblas strip I complained to my family that I wouldn't be staying there long and that I wanted to do a walk down the strip, and then go back to get on the train back to Santa Susanna. As we walked down the main central path of the strip we took many pictures, as well as stop to buy gifts for our friends and family back home. Once we had reached the end of the strip we decided to cross onto the side path in order to walk back up. I believe that this decision saved our lives. As we were walking back up to the train station, my friend said that we should all cross back over onto the middle path, but my mum stated that we couldn't as there was a shop further up on the corner that she needed to go into. I then said that I would cross over back into the middle as I wanted to purchase an ice-cream. As I was about to cross over, I looked to my left and there was an ice-cream parlour right next to me (another blessing which I believe saved my life). Within a minute of me getting my ice-cream a terrorist drove a van at high speed down the central path of the Las Ramblas, mowing down and killing 13 and injuring over a 100 people. My family and I ran into restaurants where they had to put the shutters down to protect us. During this time of being in the restaurant I didn't know what to think or feel. My adrenaline level was high, and all that I wanted to do was make sure that we were all safe. When we found out via the news channel what was happening outside, we were saddened. We were okay but there were others that had lost their lives. I really felt for the families of all those that were involved. Once we were able to leave the restaurant hours later, the bodies of those who had lost their lives were scattered on the central path around us, my soul grieved for them. I praised God that my family members were all okay even though we were all shook up. Our lives were all graciously and miraculously spared at that very moment. Continuing with our journey, we boarded the train to go back to Santa Susanna all sitting in silence recalling the events of the day; each grateful in our own individual way that we were safe. We decided once we had gotten off the train that we would go to a restaurant for food as we were all hungry. Once in the restaurant, the waiter came over to serve us. When my daughter pointed out the name on the waiter's name tag I couldn't believe my eyes. The waiters name was Jesus! Could this be coincidence? I knew it wasn't coincidence when we arrived back at our hotel and went to the bar to get some water. Once again my daughter pointed out the name of the bartender who served us. The bartenders name was Christian! I knew this was no coincidence. Jesus Christ is my Saviour which makes me a Christian! God was showing us that it was Him that protected us on that day. I was so overwhelmed and grateful. Praise God! God sure does work in mysterious ways!!!

My life has been an emotional rollercoaster, there were times when I used to think and wonder why I was experiencing the pain that I have had to feel. Times when and where, I didn't think that I was going to make it. Times where and when, I lost all hope and felt like giving up, but the LORD miraculously came into my life, and He gave me hope, He gave me joy, He gave me peace. Don't get me wrong, I am human, I still fail on many occasions, I still feel down sometimes but the difference this time is I have peace that surpasses all understanding. Peace when there is a lot of things falling apart around about me, because I know He is the Prince of Everlasting Peace – (**Jehovah Shalom**). And, His peace is eternal peace, which only the LORD can truly bring and give. Recently, as I have tried to finish this book, I have been coming up against the schemes of hell. I know that the devil does not want this book out because he knows that others will see my story of the power of deliverance, and hopefully cling to Jesus for theirs. Satan our adversary and the enemy of God, doesn't want people free. He wants people bound to their circumstances with no hope of a way out. I had been suffering with migraine headaches in the past few months of finishing this book, so I had to have a CT scan. Due to the headaches I stopped writing for about a week. Then the day that I started writing again, the anxiety flared up, and I had a panic attack on my way home from work. Afterwards, I had 3 recurring dreams that my tongue was tied with rope wrapped all around it. I know that was the LORD showing me that Satan is trying to stop my words through this book, but it just made me more determined to finish it! A dear friend, who has the gift of healing, informed me that anxiety or worry is not of God, and that it is from the enemy. He asked me if he could pray with me over the phone. As he prayed, casting away demons and stating that no demonic force has any power over me, I felt the anxiety lift. To this day I haven't had a panic attack. I also received my results for my CT scan, and they came back normal. God is good, AMEN!!!

I still sometimes feel emotional when I see little girls with their fathers playing around, and wondering why I had to grow up without a father, but as the Holy Bible states in the Book of Psalms: *"God is a Father to the fatherless!"* (Psalm 68:5)

And my story is proof of that. I no longer feel insecure and jealous of other women. I have learnt to love myself and understand who I am in Christ in God. I am comfortable in my own skin, and no longer wish that I was anybody else. I can now finally see myself through the LORD'S eyes. I no longer feel insecure in my relationship/marriage to Errol. I feel secure with Errol through my security in God. I no longer suffer with panic attacks. Naturally, I still worry everyday about my family members, and about death but that is something that the LORD is continually working on. I must trust Him completely. God has got my back! I won't lie, I never managed to curb my struggle with masturbation, and I still struggled greatly with it until after marriage. I think that my main reason of struggle was because I refused to tell people about my struggle. I battled with its hold on me most of my life, and didn't try to access any help for the addiction and hold that it had over me. After marriage it toned down but I wish I had spoken to trusted advisors and spiritual mothers about it sooner. That's something that I regret.

"The truth shall set you free!"

(John 8:32)

It's now January 2018, and here I am writing the

finishing touches to my manuscript. I began by God's
grace to write this book almost 10 years ago in the year
2008, and to now be almost finished is a satisfying
feeling. To see 'light at the end of a very long tunnel', is
most satisfactorily rewarding. I envisioned this book as a
teenager. I didn't know how or why I was going to write a
book, but I knew that I would. To see my vision manifest
into real life is an honour and a privilege. I am grateful to
the LORD, that He chose me to be the channel and living
instrument in which He would bring this book to fruition. I
just want to encourage anyone that is reading this book
that may not be in a good place right now, that may feel
that all hope is lost. Let me tell you this, the LORD Jesus
Christ is a forever life-changing God. He's changed me
from who I used to be - to who I am now. They say that a
Leopard cannot change its spots. That's true! What they
don't tell you is that God is the One who can change
them; after all, He's the One who created the Leopard
and its spots! All He asks is that we surrender our lives to
Him, and He will do the rest. When I ponder on my past,
it feels like I am thinking about a story that I have read

about someone else. I can't imagine or comprehend anymore what my life was like back then. It feels surreal. I can't even believe that all those things happened to me. I honestly feel like it was someone else. God has changed my life. My past no longer defines me. I am a brand new creation and brand new creature in God. There is hope, for He gives us **"Beauty for Ashes"**, and I Chantell Leonie Hayles, and millions of like-minded people, male and female, young and old, black or white, we are all living proof that God is the God of **"Second Chances"**!!

Isaiah 61:3 Good News for the Oppressed

61 The Spirit of the Sovereign LORD is upon me,
for the LORD has anointed me
to bring good news to the poor.
He has sent me to comfort the broken-hearted
and to proclaim that captives will be released
and prisoners will be freed.
2 He has sent me to tell those who mourn
that the time of the LORD's favour has come,
and with it, the day of God's anger against their enemies.
3 To all who mourn in Israel,

he will give a crown of beauty for ashes,
a joyous blessing instead of mourning,
festive praise instead of despair.
In their righteousness, they will be like great oaks
that the LORD has planted for his own glory.
4 They will rebuild the ancient ruins,
repairing cities destroyed long ago.
They will revive them,
though they have been deserted for many generations.
5 Foreigners will be your servants.
They will feed your flocks
and plow your fields
and tend your vineyards.
6 You will be called priests of the LORD,
ministers of our God.
You will feed on the treasures of the nations
and boast in their riches.
7 Instead of shame and dishonour,
you will enjoy a double share of honour.
You will possess a double portion of prosperity in your
land,
and everlasting joy will be yours.
8 "For I, the LORD, love justice.
I hate robbery and wrongdoing.
I will faithfully reward my people for their suffering
and make an everlasting covenant with them.
9 Their descendants will be recognized

and honoured among the nations.
Everyone will realize that they are a people
  the LORD has blessed."
[10] I am overwhelmed with joy in the LORD my God!
  For he has dressed me with the clothing of salvation
  and draped me in a robe of righteousness.
I am like a bridegroom dressed for his wedding
  or a bride with her jewels.
[11] The Sovereign LORD will show his justice to the nations
of the world.
  Everyone will praise him!
His righteousness will be like a garden in early spring,
  with plants springing up everywhere.

I have a question to ask you right now: **"How many**

people do you know who love you so much that they

would give their life for you?" I don't know anyone

except Jesus Christ of Nazareth, who not only showed

His unconditional agape Love for me personally, but He

showed it for the whole world, regardless of age, or

colour, or culture when he hung on the Cross at Calvary

Hill for all to see and experience what true Love is. This

portion of Scripture found in the **(Book of John chapter**

3, verse 16) in the New Testament, sums up the whole

of the "Gospel" of the Lord Jesus Christ in a nutshell:

"For God so loved the world that He gave His one and only Son (Jesus), that whosoever believes in Him shall not perish but have everlasting life."

Throughout the Holy Bible we are shown that God

wants a very close, personal, loving relationship with His children and intimacy with us as He had with Jesus. A father or mother will bend down to a little child, pick him up and hold him close. The child will be comforted when anxious, helped when troubled, encouraged when despondent, guided when unsure and have every need provided. Our God is doing that to us every single day. His heart is open to us, His hand outstretched, in love, and He looks for that love to be returned by us to Him. Dear reader, my prayer is that you too will experience God's Love, through His Son Jesus. God gave His only Son Jesus, to die for you personally. He shed His precious blood for you personally on the Cross, and He resurrected on the Third Day, so that you would have everlasting life personally, with Him in Heaven as He promised in the Holy Bible. Jesus Christ said in the (Book of John chapter 14 and verse 6), *"I am the Way, the Truth, and the Life. No-one comes to the Father (God) except through Me."*

And in the same book of (John, chapter 3, verse 3), Jesus also said that: *"No-one can see the kingdom of God unless he is born again."* Verse 7, Jesus spoke direct and truthful by saying, *"You must be born again."*

- (1 Peter 3: 18) says: *"For Christ died for sins once and for all, the righteous for the unrighteous to bring you to God."*

- (Acts 4:12) says: **"Salvation is found in no-one else, for there is no other name under heaven given to men**

by which we must be saved."

- (Romans 6:23) says: **"For the wages of sin is death, but the gift of God is eternal life in Christ Jesus our LORD."**

(In the same Book of Romans chapter 10, verse 9 and verse 10), it says: ***"That if you confess with your mouth, 'Jesus is LORD', and believe in your heart that God raised Him from the dead, you will be saved. For it is with your heart that you believe and are justified (just-as-if-you've-never-sinned), and it is with your mouth that you confess and are saved."***

(*Italics mine*).

My friend, unless you have peace with God, your life will always be in pieces! God wants a personal relationship with you. He wants to better your individual life, spiritually, mentally, emotionally, physically and financially. He promised us through His Son Jesus, in the **(Book of John 10:10)**, a more abundant life. In the **(Book of Matthew chapter 28:20),** Jesus promised us all, that He would be with us always, to the very end of age. Stop putting your trust in men or women, who have failed you, and let you down. Start putting your trust in someone who has never ever let any person down - Jesus Christ! All you have to do is believe in Him, accept Him as your LORD and personal Saviour, then you will obtain everlasting life that He promised us and also inherit all the blessings of God, He also promised unto all His children (believers), found in the Holy Bible. God loves *you!* In any language there are no more wonderful words. God showed us that unique unconditional love by sending His Son Jesus Christ, into the world as a man to suffer and die on the Cross in our place and rise again to conquer sin and death. Such great love requires a personal response. Today, my friend if you would like to surrender your life right now to Jesus Christ, and to have a personal everyday relationship with Him, and to make Him LORD over every situation of your life, then please repeat this sinner's prayer from your heart aloud. For Jesus promised everyone: ***"Believe in the name of the LORD Jesus, and you will be saved - you and your household."***

(Acts 16:31)

PRAYER FOR YOURSELF

*"LORD, thank you for sending Your Son Jesus to die for me on the Cross. I am turning away from my sin and rebellion today to receive Jesus Christ into my heart, and into my life right now as my personal Saviour and LORD, and my very best friend, in His name I pray." - **AMEN.***

Dear friend, if you prayed this prayer I welcome you

right now into the family of God (the Body of Christ). I pray that you will find now find a born again Christian church that believes in the Holy Bible, and the gifts of the Holy Spirit near where you live to fellowship with other fellow-minded Christians. I pray that you will purchase a Holy Bible if you don't already have one, and read it everyday. And, lastly as a Christian you must pray to God everyday!

PRAYERS FOR DELIVERANCE

Here below I have included in this book a prayer by

kind permission from Evangelist Daniele Luciano Moskal,
for the deliverance of anyone who is struggling from any
of the spirits of pornography, fornication, sexual
perversion, adultery, sexual addictions, lust and
masturbation.

"FATHER GOD ALMIGHTY,
I come to You right now in the name of Jesus Christ
of Nazareth, and I break the hold of any evil parasite
power of sexual addictions, pornography,
fornication, adultery, masturbation, and lust over my
life in Jesus Christ's anointed name, and I cast out of
my mind by the power of Jesus Christ of Nazareth,
every satanic lustful or sexual image the enemy has
sent to play on my mind . The blood of Jesus Christ
of Nazareth is against you Satan! I nullify every effect
of the serpent's bite of sexual perversion upon my

*life, in the anointed name and blood of Jesus Christ
of Nazareth! I decree and I declare by the anointed
blood of Jesus Christ of Nazareth, that every evil
stranger and all satanic deposits in my life right now,
I command you to be paralyzed and to get out of my
life right now, in the name of Jesus Christ of
Nazareth! I decree and I declare in the name of Jesus
Christ of Nazareth, that greater is HE that lives in me
than he that lives in the world! I decree and I declare
by the anointed blood of Jesus Christ of Nazareth –
my mind is the mind of Jesus Christ, and I can do all
things through Christ who strengthens me! Holy
Ghost fire, purge my mind, body and soul
completely, in the anointed name and blood of Jesus
Christ of Nazareth! I decree and declare that all these
evil spirits shall not reign in my mortal body. I shall
not obey them in any shape, way or form because I
washed thoroughly by the anointed blood of Jesus
Christ of Nazareth! I decree and I declare that my
mind, body, spirit, and my soul shall not be an
instrument of unrighteousness to sin but I present
my body to God as a living sacrifice unto God – and
sin shall have no dominion over me by the blood of*

Jesus Christ of Nazareth! I decree and I declare by the authority and power invested in me – and by the anointed blood of Jesus Christ of Nazareth my complete total deliverance from the spirit of fornication, sexual immorality, adultery, pornography, sexual perversion, lust and masturbation in the awesome name of Jesus Christ of Nazareth!

AMEN & AMEN & AMEN!!!

(Ref: Please read the Book of ROMANS chapter 6)

"PURPOSE IN THE PAIN" MINISTRIES

'**P**urpose in the **P**ain' **Ministries** greatest desire is to

bring the personal growth of God's unconditional love and acceptance, hope and encouragement, understanding and healing for crippled emotions. To bring deliverance and liberty in its simplest form to the discouraged and emotionally wounded women of this world, to show and teach them that there is contentment that overcomes depression, peace in the midst of adverse circumstances, and motivation and grace for living - that life has a purpose. The Founder of 'Purpose in the Pain Ministries', *Chantell Leonie Hayles* believes that everybody has a story that can help someone else, that through the pain, purpose can be found!!!

To contact the author for bookings or for further information with regards to this book please send an email too:

purposeinthepain.ministries@outlook.com

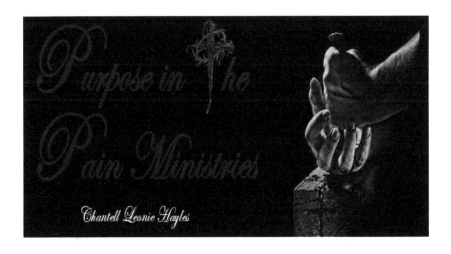

© 2018 Chantell Leonie Hayles

#0126 - 270818 - C0 - 210/148/10 - PB - DID2286697